DOING MERITOCRACY RIGHT

DOING MERITOCRACY RIGHT

How Business Leaders Can Turn an American Aspiration into Reality (and Why They Should)

THOMAS A. COLE

The University of Chicago Press
Chicago and London

The University of Chicago Press, Chicago 60637
The University of Chicago Press, Ltd., London

Published 2025
Printed in the United States of America

34 33 32 31 30 29 28 27 26 25 1 2 3 4 5

ISBN-13: 978-0-226-84457-2 (cloth)
ISBN-13: 978-0-226-84459-6 (paper)
ISBN-13: 978-0-226-84458-9 (ebook)
DOI: https://doi.org/10.7208/chicago/9780226844589.001.0001

Library of Congress Cataloging-in-Publication Data

Names: Cole, Thomas A. (Lawyer), author.
Title: Doing meritocracy right : how business leaders can turn an American aspiration into reality (and why they should) / Thomas A. Cole.
Description: Chicago : The University of Chicago Press, 2025. | Includes bibliographical references and index.
Identifiers: LCCN 2025018516 | ISBN 9780226844572 (cloth) | ISBN 9780226844596 (paperback) | ISBN 9780226844589 (ebook)
Subjects: LCSH: Equality—United States—History—21st century. | Merit (Ethics) | Civil service reform—United States. | Elite (Social sciences)—United States. | Social mobility—United States. | Business ethics—United States.
Classification: LCC HN90.S6 C63 2025 | DDC 174/.40973—dc23/eng/20250515
LC record available at https://lccn.loc.gov/2025018516

♾ This paper meets the requirements of ANSI/NISO Z39.48-1992 (Permanence of Paper).

Authorized Representative for EU General Product Safety Regulation (GPSR) queries: **Easy Access System Europe**—Mustamäe tee 50, 10621 Tallinn, Estonia, gpsr.requests@easproject.com
Any other queries: https://press.uchicago.edu/press/contact.html

Dedicated to Connie and our daughters,
sons-in-law, and grandchildren.
And dedicated to the memories of Howard Trienens and
Newton Minow, inspiring leaders and generous mentors.

CONTENTS

PREFACE

Ever since the days of Thomas Jefferson, the notion of meritocracy has played a central role in American life and, some would say, mythology.

This does not mean the institution has always been vibrant. What passed for meritocracy during the early years of the republic was objectively weak by excluding those who weren't born white, male, and (perhaps) Protestant. But even after Emancipation and women's suffrage—and with further advances, however modest, during the early 1900s and after World War II—a diluted meritocracy still prevailed. In the twenty-first century, the full implementation of an American system that places people into "positions of success, power, and influence on the basis of their demonstrated abilities and merit"—or even a system that applies a robust and demanding definition of "merit"—has remained elusive.

This failure of full attainment is not due to lack of attention to the subject. There has been a deluge of recent books about meritocracy. Podcasts on the subject abound. References to meritocracy also pop up where you least expect to find them, sometimes lampooning the notion of it as an American institution. A *New Yorker* magazine cartoon shows two smug middle-aged white men enjoying drinks by the pool, with one saying to the other "Meritocracy worked for my grandfather, it worked for my father, and it's working for me."[1]

Meritocracy is now under attack and is one of the battlegrounds in the culture wars. Some critics attack meritocracy for failing to have equality as its goal. Others attack it for being insufficiently inclusive. Indeed, some assert that we have never really achieved a meritocracy. Shortcomings in the definition of "merit" are criticized. Many critics base their attacks on the demeanor and failures of the winners of meritocracy—namely, the elite. Still others argue that the whole concept places unacceptable burdens on the elite and those who aspire to membership in the elite.

A great deal of attention—in the form of articles and services offered by consultants—has been given to actions designed to remedy insufficient inclusiveness. But many of those recommended actions had to be modified as a result of the landmark 2023 US Supreme Court decision in *Students for Fair Admissions v. Harvard* (referred to herein as the Harvard/UNC case). Indeed, the deluge of recent, largely negative commentary about affirmative action and diversity, equity, and inclusion (DEI) threatens to distract attention from a more general discussion about meritocracy. On the other hand, and paradoxically, a focus on those subjects just might encourage a broader group of people in leadership positions to think about the adjacent issues of defining merit and the demeanor of the elite. Let's hope so!

I am an unabashed supporter of meritocracy. In environments where equality of opportunity is achieved, meritocracy puts able, deserving individuals in positions of authority, thereby expanding the number of such individuals in places where society should want them.

That is not to say I disagree with some of the criticisms lodged at meritocracy. (Here I quickly ask: What system of social organization doesn't have flaws?) The solution to the problems of meritocracy is not abandonment, but reform. And, for the reasons set forth in this book, those reforms are best effected by the private sector.

After nearly half a century of advising CEOs and boards of directors, I know that there can be a limited appetite for lengthy discourse—especially on a subject that may not be perceived to be directly related to significant and challenging day-to-day responsibilities. So, I start as I often did during decades of providing advice to corporate leaders: I will give you the short version here; read beyond this preface to get the long version.

The short version is this: A meritocratic society is achieved in two, interrelated stages. The first is access to quality education; the second is access to post-education promotion (and with it, to membership in the elite—positions of power, financial reward, and prestige). The proper goal of meritocracy is delivering access to these stages—to promote equal opportunity, not equality. Equal opportunity should be achieved by elevating access to opportunities for the disadvantaged, not by eliminating opportunities for the privileged. Elevating opportunity may require structures of equity—different levels of support, based on needs—to ensure that everyone has a chance to climb the ladder. With such structures, societies create, and benefit from, a system in which individual talents shine through. Meritocracy is not the cause of poverty and rising income inequality, nor is it more than a partial solution to these problems (even with reforms that increase opportunities).

Two significant flaws in the current application of meritocracy have made the principle more fraught than necessary. First, there exist continuing barriers to giving every deserving person a reasonable shot at being considered based on their merits and in an environment of equal opportunity. Some would label this a failure of inclusion, attributable to insufficient attention to equity, to meritocratic inheritance (a modern form of aristocracy), to credentialism, and to the lingering effects of systemic racism. Each of these problems is true, as far as they go. But attempts to remediate such failures of inclusion too often fall exclusively to affirmative action and

DEI programs—initiatives whose impact, efficacy, and acceptance have been made all the more challenging following the Harvard/UNC case. Also challenging, but no less important, is to implement those programs without applying a double standard in assessing individuals.

The second significant flaw is a definition of merit that is too narrow, failing to adequately apply criteria that relate to character and to look beyond simple metrics when considering who deserves membership in the elite. Here is where the most significant failings of many who are among the elite emerge, especially hubris and condescension. Those characteristics, coupled with some spectacularly bad and consequential decisions by those in leadership positions, have led to a loss of respect for authority and fed demagoguery.

Against this landscape, leadership of the private sector, rather than the government, has greatest capacity to effect change and lead the effort for reform. For individuals across corporate America, much can be learned from the best practices of professional services firms—law firms, management consultants, accounting firms, and investment banks—which out of necessity have taken significant steps designed to address the flaws and failings just described.

Finally, the leadership of the private sector can and should exert influence beyond the four walls of their businesses. Those leaders can address the meritocratic shortcomings of universities, governments, and communities, even if those efforts might yield only marginal improvements. But given how both business organizations and society at large will benefit from a reformed meritocracy, and with this book's argument that private-sector leaders are the most suitable vessels for such change, it is incumbent on those in the elite to carry the mantle of meritocracy forward.

The long version—but not too long a version—occupies the rest of this book. I provide support for each of the positions set forth in the short version, lay out some pertinent history, explain some key concepts, and discuss some of the most controversial issues. I hope that you, reader, will take the time to dive into the long version. Achieving a meritocratic society requires a full appreciation for the complexity of the subject and a recognition that executing well on the best of intentions requires immersion in the issues' larger context. I hope readers in a position to help do meritocracy right will be convinced to exercise their influence and to effect reform at all levels. To facilitate those efforts, I set forth a "to-do list" for reform at the end of this book.

INTRODUCTION

Meritocracy is defined as "a system, organization, or society in which people are chosen and moved into positions of success, power, and influence on the basis of their demonstrated abilities and merit."[1] Another definition rounds out the point with ". . . not because of their money or social position."[2]

Individuals who achieve positions of success, power, and influence—the winners in a meritocracy—are referred to, and occasionally derided as, "the elite." These individuals—the social elite—are different from, say, top athletes and virtuoso musicians, among others, who are labeled "elite" based on their success in their chosen fields. Compared to an elite athlete or musician (even Taylor Swift!), a member of the *social* elite has greater capacity to exert power and influence over others. The social elite are most commonly, and in the scope of this book, the leaders of organizations in the private sector.

Utilization of an appropriate definition of merit is perhaps the most important task in achieving a true meritocracy. It has a positive impact on inclusiveness, as well as on the quality of those who will occupy positions of power and influence. A meritocratic society requires that meritocracy be fairly implemented in each of two stages—in access to quality education; and in post-education advancement to positions of power, wealth, and prestige.

A first cousin of meritocracy is the American Dream, defined as "a social order in which each man and each woman shall be able to attain the fullest stature of which they are innately capable, and to be recognized by others for what they are, regardless of the fortuitous circumstances of birth or position."[3] The availability of the American Dream to persons regardless of race has been a challenge. Abraham Lincoln in 1860 said, "I want every man to have a chance—and I believe a Black man is entitled to it—in which he can better his condition—when he may look forward and hope to be a hired laborer this year and the next, work for himself afterward, and finally hire men to work for him! That is the true system."[4] And yet, over one hundred years later, Dr. Martin Luther King Jr. was still dreaming of the day when people "will not be judged by the color of their skin but by the content of their character."[5]

While meritocracy and the American Dream are cousins, there is a difference. The latter allows citizens to "attain the fullest stature of which they are innately capable," while the former determines who will be members of the elite. Nevertheless, one of the steps to reform meritocracy—making it more inclusive through greater equality of opportunity—will also revitalize the American Dream.

Ironically, the term "meritocracy" was coined as "a derisive term for a new system of class oppression" by Alan Fox, writing in *Socialist Commentary* in May 1956.[6] (The origin of the term is more frequently attributed to Michael Young, the author of the 1958 satire called *The Rise of the Meritocracy*.)[7] Despite Fox and Young, for most of the second half of the twentieth century, meritocracy was credited with the positive connotations described in the definitions quoted in the first paragraph. Moreover, the notion of organizing society in an anti-aristocratic fashion long preceded the coining of the term. Indeed, it is part of the origin story of our republic.

Meritocracy is like other principles of social organization—democracy, capitalism, the rule of law—in that the quality of execution is never perfect and the extent of achieving its goals can ebb and flow over time. Some of the flaws in the execution of meritocracy were present mid-twentieth century. A foremost example is the exclusion of many women and minorities (and even non-Protestants) from being assessed on the merits, from being part of the system, and from being given a fair shot at achieving the American Dream, much less joining the elite. Other flaws developed over that time period—the definition of "merit" became too limited; the pursuit of the rewards of meritocracy was gamed by the wealthy, with greater consequences when income and wealth gaps expanded and "credentialism" loomed larger. As a result, "meritocratic inheritance," the modern version of aristocracy, grew.

The flaws in execution were evidenced in some spectacular and consequential failures on the part of the elite. It was the "best and brightest" and the "smartest people in the room" who brought us the Vietnam War, Watergate, the savings and loan crisis, Enron's bankruptcy, the wars in Iraq and Afghanistan, the global financial crisis, and the opioid epidemic. And it was the elite who helped promote, and were taken in by, Madoff, Theranos, and FTX. Too many in the elite engaged in behavior that led to the #MeToo movement. Some in the elite are alleged to benefit from "crony capitalism" and engage in "rent seeking."[8]

Despite these failures, many in the elite have seemed to become more arrogant and out of touch. Some of the wealthiest of the elite fostered this impression by being the embodiment of Veblen's "conspicuous consumption"—with superyachts, private jets, and homes (sometimes multiple homes) featured in *The Wall Street Journal*'s Friday "Mansion" section. And then, there is what might be called "conspicuous compensation" of the elite in business—the sometimes-breathtaking compensation of the CEOs of public companies. The amounts are large in absolute dollars and, also, in comparison to the median compensation of all employees. Both the amounts and the comparisons are "conspicuous" because they are required to be disclosed under rules of the Securities and Exchange Commission, the latter disclosure labeled "pay ratio."

Two aspects of CEO compensation seem to be underappreciated by those who criticize it. First, it is heavily driven by stock price appreciation, and a majority of US households also benefit because they own public company equity, either directly or indirectly. Second, many entertainers and athletes make similar amounts and lead even more lavish lifestyles while providing fewer meaningful societal benefits. But they never seem to be criticized as arrogant, out of touch, or overcompensated. In fact, the astronomical compensation of some entertainers and athletes is sometimes lauded. Case in point: See the June 2024 article about three NBA players with the headline "$100 Million a Year . . . and Worth Every Penny!"[9]

Others have noted that the elite frequently direct their condescension at those who are less educated and especially those who live in rural America. *Demon Copperhead*, Barbara Kingsolver's Appalachian-based update of *David Copperfield*, includes these observations: "The ones in charge started cooking it into everybody's brains to look down on the land people [that is, those in rural America], saying we are an earlier stage of human life" and "words have been flung like pieces of shit, only to get stuck on a truck bumper with up-yours pride. Rednecks, moonshiners, ridge runners, hicks. Deplorables."[10] Lest these quotes seem overly dramatic, remember the use of that last word in the 2016 presidential election and consider the success of anti-elite demagogues in garnering votes in rural counties. As John Cochrane put it so well, "there's no better way to stick it to the elites than to vote for the man [Trump] who drives them most crazy."[11] Others in the elite were literally allowed to be out of touch as a result of being beneficiaries (sometimes gloating beneficiaries) of the "velvet rope economy."[12] This is Nelson Schwartz's term for business models that allow the elite to purchase or otherwise receive priority treatment. Examples include luxury "skyboxes" at stadiums around the country, the Disney World Genie+ pass and the United Airlines Global Services status. Becoming the patient of a primary care physician on a "concierge" basis is another example.

One of the best stories about arrogance on the part of the elite involves a self-important airline passenger who, unhappy with a gate agent, thundered, "Do you know who I am?!." The agent calmly said, "one moment, sir," picked up her paging microphone and announced to the terminal: "There is a man at gate _ who apparently is suffering from amnesia; if you are missing someone from your party, please come here to assist."

Those failures and arrogance have led to a loss of respect for authority and have fed demagoguery. This was recognized by none other than Steve Bannon. His explanation for the recent successes of populist and ultraright-wing politicians was that the elites "are more and more detached from the lived experiences of their people."[13]

In addition, recent experience with meritocracy has unleashed a flood of criticism. It has been observed that "criticism [of meritocracy] now crosses the political spectrum from the social-democratic left to the populist right."[14] The other recent books on the subject—and there are many of them (see appendix A)—take a decidedly negative view of meritocracy. Their titles use terms like "tyranny"[15] and "myth,"[16] and they describe the winners in a meritocracy as "snobby cosmopolitans"[17] engaged in a "charade"[18] of making the world a better place. Meritocracy is called a "sham" and a "trap" that turns "every colleague [into] a competitor"[19] and an "alibi for plutocracy."[20] It has been called an "ideological myth to obscure and extend economic and social inequalities."[21] It has been accused of "promoting a socially corrosive ethic of competitive self-interest,"[22] even to the point of promoting cheating. David Brooks has asserted that "meritocracy's utilitarian, instrumentalist mindset can, in some cases, distort a sacred bond: parenthood" creating "meritocratic [as opposed to 'simple'] affection" in which "some parents unconsciously shape their expressions of love to steer their children toward behavior they think will lead to achievement and happiness."[23]

Despite the fact that the notion has been around forever, it has been called the "ideological engine of late capitalism."[24] Perhaps the most pessimistic of all assessments was this—"There is reason to doubt that even a perfectly realized meritocracy would be a just society."[25]

The American Dream has received similar criticism. It has been called a "foundational myth" that puts too much emphasis on "individual determination, brittle self-sufficiency, and personal accomplishment," detracting from "robust social programs that would address root causes" of social ills.[26] A more whimsical criticism is George Carlin's pithy comment: "They call it the American Dream, because you have to be asleep to believe it."[27] Finally, David Leonhardt in his recent book *Ours Was the Shining Future* laments "the decline of the American Dream over the past half century." He attributes that decline to "the lack of a strong political movement dedicated to protecting that dream," resulting in the abandonment of "democratic capitalism," which he defines as "a system in which the government recognizes its crucial role in guiding the economy." Leonhardt contrasts "democratic capitalism" with "rough-and-tumble capitalism."[28] I agree with Leonhardt that some degree of governmental regulation of the economy is needed. However, I believe that revitalizing the American Dream is best achieved not by increased regulation of businesses, but rather as a by-product of one of the steps to reform meritocracy—greater inclusiveness—and look to the private sector to take on that task.

All of the authors of the recent books are academics or journalists. I confess that I, too, come at the subject in part from an academic perspective. I have taught a law school seminar on corporate governance and a seminar for undergrads on organizational leadership. My teaching and writing have emphasized organizational decision-making. Deciding whom to hire and promote, and how to mentor, train, retain, and compensate people, are among the most critical decisions in any organization. Boards are now expected to focus on talent management. The selection of a CEO is perhaps the acid test of the commitment to meritocracy on the part of any organization, whether for-profit or not-for-profit.

My perspective is not limited to the academic, however. I had the privilege of serving for decades in a leadership position in a large, global law firm. I have also been a counselor and adviser to a large number of public corporations (and their CEOs and boards) in a wide variety of industry sectors. I have served as a director or trustee of numerous not-for-profit institutions, including one of the so-called Ivy-plus universities, as well as one of the top academic medical centers in the US. All of that has given me a real-world perspective on how meritocracy is practiced, how that practice has changed over the past forty or more years and how it can be improved. It has given me an overall optimistic view of business and professional organizations and respect for their leaders.

These academic and the practical perspectives (and my own experience as a beneficiary of meritocracy) cause me to be an unapologetic cheerleader for the concept . . . and yet a strong advocate for its reform and for the revitalization of the American Dream. Why a cheerleader and why reform? A well-functioning meritocracy (that is, one that has been reformed in the manner discussed in this book) will increase the talent available to lead our important institutions and will place leadership in the hands of humble individuals of good character and high integrity. This will yield benefits at both the organizational and societal level, as discussed in chapter 9.

And even though I believe meritocracy is in need of reform, I don't blame the current, unreformed version of meritocracy for rising economic inequality and stagnation in upward mobility. Those, I believe, are caused by factors other than meritocracy, even with its current flaws. Those other factors include the lingering effects of systemic racism, technology and automation without worker retraining, a decline in apprenticeship programs and vocational schools, a decline in the influence of labor unions, the ascent of the Chinese economy, outsourcing and the gig economy that eliminates the corporate ladder for many, and pressure from shareholder activists for short-term results. Finally, Nicholas Kristof, writing in *The New York Times* in 2023 and citing a recent book by Melissa Kearney entitled *The Two-Parent Privilege*, observed that "the breakdown of the family primarily among low-income Americans may be uncomfortable to talk about, but it is part of the apparatus of inequality in the United States."[29]

Meritocracy as currently practiced in the post-education stage is in need of reform in three critical aspects. In order to achieve greater equality of opportunity (the appropriate goal), it needs to be more inclusive through, among other things, less meritocratic inheritance; less credentialism; and continuing attention to affirmative action and to diversity, equity, and inclusion (albeit with some possible modifications due to the recent decision in the Harvard/UNC case). The definition of merit—which determines who is worthy of joining the elite and thus creates incentives for specified behaviors—needs to be expanded and thoughtfully applied. Finally, those who are admitted to the elite need to be more humble and less condescending. They need to recognize that their successes were attributable, in part, to the contributions of others and simple good fortune. That "attitude adjustment" will serve both the individuals and their organizations well.

Even among those who agree that there is a need to reform meritocracy, there is controversy over whether that task should be undertaken by the government or the private sector. That debate is discussed in chapter 5. Spoiler alert! (Actually not much of a spoiler, given the subtitle of this book.) I believe firmly that reform should be led by leaders in the private sector—starting with actions taken within their own organizations. Leaders in the private sector (both current and retired) can and should also contribute to reforming meritocracy in education and government. They can and should push for improvements in their communities that will open doors, and remove impediments, to equal opportunity.

As noted in the preface, a principal target audience of this book is the leadership of corporate America. The term "corporate America" is not limited to large publicly traded companies, although they often have an outsized impact on society. That said, private companies provide employment for a much larger number of citizens (in the aggregate), a number of private companies are quite large and many of leaders of private companies (regardless of size) are men and women who have the potential to exert significant influence outside of their own organizations. Thus, this book is directed at all who are in leadership positions in corporate America (broadly defined). It is also directed at those who aspire to be in the next generation of those leaders.

The goal is to inform and persuade current and future leaders about how and why to reform meritocracy. In writing about John Lewis and the struggle for civil rights, Jon Meacham observed that "change in America most often comes when the powerless attract the attention of the powerful."[30] How can we "attract the attention of the powerful" (i.e., the leaders of the private sector) and convince them to participate in the reform effort?

I start by recognizing that leaders in the private sector are very busy running their organizations and addressing a variety of challenges (supply chain issues, disruptive innovation from competitors, the effects of inflation, short-term orientation of many of their investors, and so on). As a result, many of those leaders (like me when I was preoccupied with leading a law firm) haven't taken much time to think deeply about meritocracy or read the many recent books on the subject. Thus, a first step is to provide a bit of a primer about meritocracy—its history, key concepts and areas of controversy. That is the purpose of part I of this book.

The next step is to convince the leaders that there are benefits to be enjoyed by their own organizations from reformed meritocracy and, further, that this is a complex subject and an intuitive approach is not sufficient. For an effective meritocracy, much more is needed than simply picking from an already available pool of talent "the best person for the job," especially if "best person" is determined using a wholly inadequate definition of merit. From observation and experience, I believe that the large professional services firms—out of necessity—have developed some best practices, albeit with mixed results, that nevertheless can be adopted and amplified by corporate America. That is the subject of part II, which also addresses one of the most vital applications of meritocracy in corporate America—CEO succession. Part II also explains how private-sector leaders can influence universities to take steps that will enhance meritocracy, what they should do to help populate government with meritorious officials, and how they can lead their communities to take steps that will increase equality of opportunity.

Finally, anticipating that some readers might ask, "Why bother?" part III addresses the benefits that could, and hopefully will, result from a reformation of meritocracy.

One last point of introduction: It is probably my decades of advising public companies about disclosure requirements that compel me to set out my own experiences with meritocracy so that the reader can reach his or her own conclusions about my possible biases in addressing the subject. Here goes.

I first heard the term "meritocracy" in the late 1970s from a fellow associate in our law firm's Chicago office. He was leaving to move back home to Kentucky to help his family deal with some serious issues. He said that he would miss the firm, because "it is the closest thing that I know of to a perfect meritocracy." He may have been reflecting on the fact that he and I (among others) had come from modest backgrounds with no "network," and yet we were both thriving professionally. This, in contrast with the less favorable prospects of a couple of our fellow associates who almost certainly would not have been hired on their own merits but were the children of senior executives of major clients. To both of us, the concept of meritocracy seemed an unassailably good thing.

We, of course, held that point of view without much deep thought on the subject. While we came from modest backgrounds, we were both straight white Christian men who had attended decent suburban public schools (mine was about half college prep in non–Main Line Philadelphia). In the late 1950s, my school district had placed me into a "gifted student" track, with a heavy emphasis on science and math beginning in late elementary school. (I have always believed this was a reaction to the Soviet launch of Sputnik!) My fellow associate and I had somehow managed to get ourselves admitted to selective universities and law schools. We were not particularly concerned about the fact that many of our classmates in higher education had been "legacy admittees," had applications flagged by a development office, or had benefited from superior secondary educations at public schools in very affluent areas or at private prep schools.

Nor, frankly, did we pause to consider the fact that our individual merit was being judged within a system that, at the time, was being applied to only a subset of the population. For example, in 1975, the year I graduated from law school, women constituted only 20 percent of law students, and 7.8 percent of law students were members of minorities. At the time, openly LGBTQ individuals were largely outside the system. We were not so many years past the enactment of the Civil Rights Act of 1964 and the discrimination that had continued thereafter. For example, "redlining" was not outlawed until 1968, and the Equal Credit Opportunity Act did not get enacted until 1974. Nevertheless, because the system of meritocracy had included and rewarded us, and we had our heads down trying to succeed in a new career, there was neither the inclination nor time for us to question the system.

Years later, when I was serving in a leadership position in our law firm (a position attained, in no small measure, as a matter of luck!),

I was intuitively focused on making decisions about our colleagues based on merit, and I did consider "character" and "collegiality" to be important elements of merit. I was explicitly focused on addressing only one other aspect of meritocracy—namely, increasing the pool of talent through diversity. (During my time serving in as a leader of the firm, we won the Catalyst Award in recognition of our efforts to advance the careers of our women lawyers; formed our diversity committee; and started our pipeline program, the Sidley Prelaw Scholars.)

Finally, as will be discussed in chapter 2, I advocate including life experience as an element of the definition of merit, no doubt because of my own experiences. I was sometimes asked by law students during the interview process a rather canned question: "What experiences best prepared you for the practice of law?" I surprised many of them with my answers. I said "waiting tables," because it taught me the importance of responsiveness and service. (Katie Roiphe, writing in *The Wall Street Journal*, described the benefits of working in a restaurant even more broadly as "a master class in human interaction" and says that "learning to navigate people is something you need in every profession."[31]) I also said "working with disturbed adolescents in a residential treatment center." I explained that the experience taught me how to negotiate without a shred of leverage. And it certainly taught me humility. On reflection, I should have also mentioned "working as unskilled labor on a construction crew during summers in college." That taught me enormous respect for the skilled trades, and I also learned not to make assumptions about backgrounds of others. I recall eating lunch next to a dump truck driver who started quoting Shakespeare. His comment, on seeing the startled look on my face, was, "You never know, do you?"

Beyond those personal experiences from my youth were observations from my years in law firm management. In particular, I am thinking about a comparison of two individuals. The first came from an affluent family, with strong connections and Ivy League college and law school diplomas. The second grew up in one of the toughest neighborhoods on the South Side of Chicago, had a first career in public accounting, and then went to law school. It was the second individual who made far greater contributions to the firm and its clients. He became a member of our executive committee and, because of his extraordinary people skills and ability to assess talent, chaired our associate compensation committee.

I

MERITOCRACY 101

1

A BRIEF HISTORY OF OUR IMPERFECT MERITOCRACY

The notion of meritocracy long predated the coining of the term in the 1950s. While meritocracy today is applied in two stages—access to quality education, then post-education promotion to positions of power resulting in financial reward and prestige—the original application of the term was associated with selection of leaders in government. And government was the focus of Michael Young's 1958 satire. Hence, the combining form "-ocracy."

Plato's *Republic*, written around 375 BCE, is widely viewed as advocating meritocracy—via rule by "philosopher-kings."[1] Through various dynasties beginning around 600 CE and continuing until the beginning of the twentieth century, imperial China selected individuals for its bureaucracy based on merit, as determined in the results of civil service exams that were open to males of any class.[2] In 1813, following the separation of the American colonies from aristocratic England, Thomas Jefferson wrote to John Adams, describing a "natural aristocracy among men" based on "virtue and talent."[3] This was in contrast to "an artificial aristocracy founded on wealth and birth." He went on to write that " the form of government is the best which provides the most effectually for a pure selection of these natural aristoi into the offices of government" and that "the artificial aristocracy is a mischievous ingredient in government."[4]

The Jeffersonian ideal was, of course, limited in application to white men. The abolition of slavery in the mid-1800s did not open up access for Black people to the "natural aristocracy," in part because even white abolitionists held supremacist beliefs.[5] Systemic racism prevailed, as evidenced by Jim Crow laws and the US Supreme Court's blessing of "separate but equal" in *Plessy v. Ferguson* (1896).[6] The Pendleton Act of 1883 "established a merit-based system of selecting [federal] governmental officials and supervising their work" and was a reaction to the "spoils system," but it did not prohibit racial discrimination.[7] Indeed, racism in government received a presidential imprimatur when Woodrow Wilson authorized segregation in the federal government in 1913. He also premiered *The Birth of a Nation* at the White House in 1915. That film has been called "the most reprehensively racist film in Hollywood history."[8] The second heyday of the Ku Klux Klan (1915–1944) resulted in some local and state governments being infiltrated by white supremacists.[9] The 1925 Army War College Report on the "proposed plan for the use of Negro Manpower," among other things concluded that "compared to the white man he is admittedly of inferior mentality . . . inherently weak in character."[10] And then there was the tragedy of the "Tuskegee Study of Untreated Syphilis in the Negro Male" run by the US Public Health Service from 1932 to 1972.[11] Restrictive covenants in property deeds that were enforced by courts, as well as federal policy effectively mandating real estate redlining, suppressed the ability of Black people to build wealth through investment in residential real estate throughout much of the middle of the twentieth century. These governmental actions make it hard to argue against applying the label "systemic racism" to how society was operating in those days.

And then there were the too common racist actions of individuals. There were the vicious attacks on Black citizens, including the 1921 Tulsa Race Massacre, and there was a need for *The Negro Motorist Green Book* (published from 1936 to 1966) to safely guide Black people who were taking a road trip through the South. Zakaria has summarized this state of affairs: "The supposed midcentury utopia—with low inequality and little political polarization—was built on racial exclusion," and the two political parties "had tacitly agreed not to challenge the foundations of white supremacy."[12]

Higher education had elements of an artificial aristocracy, through the exclusion of many minorities and even poor white people. In 1901, the College Entrance Examination Board introduced a standardized test that was "intended to identify more public school students" for admission to private colleges. When the test "led to a rapid increase in 'socially undesirable' students from poor and immigrant backgrounds," as well as a "substantial growth in the number of Jewish students,"[13] the colleges reacted. They "abandoned exam-dependent admissions processes in favor of a holistic, character-based one that considered test scores as one factor among many and introduced preferences for legacies."[14] In 1922, then-President of Harvard University A. Lawrence Lowell said, "Where Jews become numerous, they drive off other people."[15] (This was quoted in a recent ad by Brandeis University, celebrating its founding in 1948 as a haven for Jewish students.)

Access to quality education based on merit, rather than wealth and birth, received a boost in 1933 by Harvard University, under the leadership of James Conant. To diversify the student body beyond white male Protestants from affluent families, Conant (the first in his family to attend college) utilized the standardized entrance exam that was the successor to the College Board—the Scholastic Aptitude Test. Nevertheless, legacy admissions continued under Conant and quotas that limited the number of students that were to be admitted from certain groups also continued. The renaming of the test in 1994 as the Scholastic *Assessment* Test was in recognition that it measures more than native intelligence and focuses on educational achievements. (This is also clearly the case with Advanced Placement tests.)

The GI Bill, enacted in 1944, was "part of a succession of meritocratic initiatives."[16] It opened the doors to higher education for returning servicemen, a significant number of whom would otherwise not have received a college education. (The Higher Education Act of 1965 further increased availability of college educations to students from lower income families by making federal funds available through what are now known as "Pell Grants.")

Nevertheless, in the second half of the twentieth century, "private colleges . . . continued to struggle balancing democratic and meritocratic ideals with aristocratic traditions."[17]

Even before the impact of the GI Bill, WWII can be thought of as a socioeconomic melting pot that helped break down class barriers, arguably with the effect of facilitating meritocracy. As Tom Brokaw writes in *The Greatest Generation*, men and women "left their ranches in Sully County, South Dakota, their jobs on the main street of Americus, Georgia, they gave up their place on the assembly lines of Detroit and in the ranks of Wall Street, they quit school or went from cap and gown directly into uniform."[18] A similar picture was painted by Buzz Bissinger in *The Mosquito Bowl*: "Brooklyn boys," "Southerners," "stoic Midwesterners," "self-collected Westerners," and "Ivy League Easterners" "came together in the great pot of World War II and learned that their differences were far less than their commonalities. They trusted one another. They learned respect for one another."[19]

The early decades of the postwar era have been described as the age of entitlement, a period of "excessive optimism."[20] The notion of a "corporate ladder" and opportunities for entrepreneurship were the vehicles for attaining upward mobility, enhanced by the "spectacular and unexpected nature of the early postwar boom."[21] Those employed by corporate America in this period had a sense of career that went beyond simply holding a job. And the term "gig" was used mostly to refer to engagement of jazz musicians.

Since those early postwar decades, real and legitimate concerns have developed about flaws in how meritocracy operates in providing access to quality education and in attaining important positions in the post-education period—ingredients of upward mobility. How did we get here?

To begin with, some of the flaws from the pre-WWII period continued in place. The socioeconomic melting pot described had limited applicability. Jim Crow reigned in a large portion of our country. Racial segregation in the military was not formally ended until 1948 by Executive Order 9981 and, to a degree, continued informally for some time thereafter. (The military has become one of our most meritocratic institutions—no doubt enhancing our national security.) Opportunities for women opened up during WWII out of necessity (e.g., Rosie the Riveter), but when men returned from the war, many of those opportunities closed again so that "the returning veterans could be reemployed. The exception was the 'pink collar' workforce."[22] The disgrace of *Plessy* was not overturned until 1954 with *Brown v. Board of Education*.[23] And even then, desegregation of public schools was resisted. For example, in 1957 in Little Rock, Arkansas, the then governor of the state acted to prevent the enrollment of Black students until President Eisenhower intervened. Many top universities did not admit Black students, and when they ultimately did so, were not particularly welcoming.[24]

Additional flaws developed over time.

The melting pot of WWII was not replicated during the Vietnam War. Children of affluence were able to avoid being drafted and sent to the war zone due to college deferments, political connections that got them into state-side reserve units, and friendly family doctors who could assist with medical deferments. As a result, "American forces in Vietnam were 55 percent working-class [and] 25 percent poor." African Americans, who were 12 percent of the general population, represented 31 percent of ground combat battalions and suffered 24 percent of the US Army's casualties.[25]

The wealthy figured out how to game the system of college admissions. Exams that were designed to create opportunities across the economic spectrum gave rise to prep courses. The Kaplan Company, while founded in 1938, went national in 1970. The Princeton Review was founded in 1980. The expense of these courses meant that the advantages they would provide would largely be available to children of affluence. Those children could afford to take the test multiple times if they were dissatisfied with their scores. The affluent were also observed to be more effective in obtaining special accommodations, such as more time, for test takers. The correlation between income and SAT scores was shown in a recent study by Opportunity Insights, a group of Harvard economists. Their study concludes that "one-third of the children from the very richest families [the top 0.1 percent] scored a 1300 or higher on the SAT, while less than 5 percent of middle-class students did," and only 0.6 percent of students from families in the bottom 20 percent achieved a score of 1300 or higher.[26]

A number of efforts have been made to neutralize these advantages. The College Board introduced an "adversity index" in 2019. That index numerically adjusted SAT scores based on socioeconomic factors. As a result of significant adverse reactions, that index was abandoned and replaced with a more qualitative assessment called Landscape.[27]

Another palliative has been introduced by universities themselves—the adoption of "test-optional" policies by more than 80 percent of colleges. These policies allow the universities to admit students who would otherwise apply with relatively low scores (as might be the case of students without access to prep courses) and include those students in an entering class without having their *U.S. News* rankings penalized by reporting lower average scores. These policies, however, may anomalously make resistance to meritocratic inheritance more difficult. As the president of Johns Hopkins University observed, "for those universities that have sought to discipline predictable pressures from well-heeled or influential parents by invoking test scores as an objective reason for admissions denials, the loss of standardized testing deepens the risk that they will be less able to resist those demands." He observed further that absence of testing might contribute to grade inflation at secondary schools.[28]

Other issues have been raised about test-optional policies, starting with whether those policies help or hinder the admissions chances of low-income students. When MIT reversed course in 2024 and became one of the first universities (followed in fairly short order by Dartmouth, Yale, Harvard, Caltech, and Brown, among others) to reinstate test requirements, its dean of admissions stated "our research shows standardized tests . . . help us identity socioeconomically disadvantaged students who lack access to advanced coursework or other enrichment opportunities that would otherwise demonstrate their readiness for MIT" and "by using the tests as a tool . . . we have helped improve the diversity of our undergraduate population." It may be that school with reputations like MIT (and the others) are simply not concerned about the possibility that reporting lower average test scores might impact their *U.S. News* rankings.[29]

Test-optional policies have become a battleground in the culture wars. According to one commentator, it "remains to be seen if [the abandonment of tests is] a marker on the road to the meritocracy's demise" and that "there are reasons to be doubtful" that the policies "will open more opportunities for the meritorious poor and middle class."[30] The migration of the elimination of test scores from colleges to medical schools triggered this reaction—"When colleges started making the SAT optional, some of us shrugged and said, well, that's fine, so long as they don't eliminate the tests for would-be brain surgeons. Now the battle lines have shifted in the meritocracy wars so that it's precisely would-be brain surgeons whose test scores the medical schools want to conceal."[31]

On top of prep courses, there developed an industry of private college counselors catering to children of affluence. They typically charge fees averaging from $4,000 to $6,000.[32] According to one firm's website, its consultants will provide "private counseling starting as early as eighth grade" covering items such as a "reading list and vocabulary program: geared toward standardized test prep," "year-by-year strategy for standardized testing," "assistance with the Common Application essays, activity sheet, awards, and background information," and "interview prep: alumni and on campus."[33]

Perhaps the most extreme versions of private college counseling were described in two recent articles. The first was a *New York Magazine* piece entitled "Inventing the Perfect College Applicant." The article profiled a twenty-eight-year-old Yale graduate whose consulting firm has 190 clients and charges clients $120,000 a year to "turn any student into Ivy bait."[34] The second article, entitled "The Guru Saying He Can Get Your 11-Year-Old into Harvard," appeared on the front page of *The Wall Street Journal*. (The editors and the guru market to the same demographic.) The guru is a twenty-nine-year-old Rhodes scholar who cofounded Crimson Education. According to the article, clients are charged from $30,000 to $200,000 for a four- to six-year program. Crimson, supported by private equity, is "now valued at $554 million."[35]

Some colleges made further accommodations for the children of wealthy families. One of the most notorious was Duke's program (since ceased) called "development admits."[36] Some version of this preferential treatment has been reported to continue at various highly selective colleges.[37] And of course there were the literally criminal activities swept up in Operation Varsity Blues. The extension of this gaming of the admissions system into the second stage of meritocracy was amplified by "credentialism" (to be discussed in the next chapter).

Another flaw has been the narrowing of the definition of "merit." The Jeffersonian ideal of virtue took a subsidiary role and the definition was too often limited to "talent plus effort." One can speculate that, in corporate America, this was a short-sighted reaction to increased pressure on short-term profits. An individual's contribution to the short-term financial success of an organization often seems to have eclipsed character in importance. On occasion, it may have led

CEOs and even boards of directors to "look the other way" when issues have been raised about the character of otherwise high performing employees. The consequence of this limitation was seen, perhaps most vividly, in the events that led to the #MeToo movement.

Finally, the elite were observed to be condescending and have been criticized for failing to recognize that their successes were attributable to luck, the contributions of colleagues, and (in many cases) the accident of birth. Too many were "born on third base, but believe they had hit a triple." When the elite feel that they have "earned" their success, they can convey a suggestion that those who are not successful deserve their plight.[38] The elite should consider the answer that investing legend Charlie Munger gave to the question: "What do you think of people who attribute their success solely to their own brilliance and hard work?" His answer: "I think that's nonsense."[39] And Jessi Streib, a Duke University sociology professor, in her study of entry-level positions for mid-tier jobs, has coined the term "luckocracy" stating that "those who win are those who guess well."[40]

2

MERIT, MORE BROADLY

A full understanding of meritocracy, and how to reform its current application, requires an appreciation of some key definitions and concepts. Achieving greater inclusiveness (a critical element of reform) and doing so in an appropriate manner requires a thoughtful consideration of affirmative action and related subjects, to be discussed in the next chapter.

DEFINING MERIT

In simplest terms, meritocracy rewards merit. One observer has noted that meritocracy creates incentives for "the activities that generate good consequences" and that "the concept of 'merit' is deeply contingent on our views of a good society." Merit needs to be defined "in the context of contemporary objectives and concerns."[1] Utilizing an appropriate and robust definition of merit is required for the achievement of a true meritocracy.

Thomas Jefferson's version was "talent plus virtue." In more recent times, merit was defined as "talent plus effort." It is regrettable that "virtue" (or a more modern word "integrity") has been essentially eliminated from the definition. It is also regrettable how "talent" came to be understood. In higher education, the assessment of talent has been too heavily dependent on grade point averages and test scores (SAT and AP, then GRE, MCAT, and LSAT). For purposes of hiring and promotion by many employers, views of talent were excessively dependent on "credentials"—and not just a four-year college diploma and, perhaps, one from a professional school. There was a premium placed on having them come from the "right" schools (the "Ivy plus" colleges and the highest ranked professional schools).

One path for reforming meritocracy is to develop, and apply, a more robust definition of "merit." Such a definition will go a long way toward addressing some of the flaws in our current approach to meritocracy. The guiding principle for drafting such a definition should be to determine the attributes that individuals should be encouraged to develop and exhibit, because individuals with such attributes will deserve to be put into positions of "success, power, and influence," and because their organizations and society at large will benefit from having them in those positions.

So, what are the elements of that robust definition of merit?

Talent—Raw intelligence is an inevitable starting point for assessing talent in just about any field of human endeavor. But that is just a starting point. It is important to recognize that talent must, and should, be developed—through education, training, and mentoring. Development of talent in corporate America requires investment in individuals by their organizations. When that investment is made on an equitable basis, equality of opportunity is enhanced, and the pool of talent is expanded. Of course, individuals need to be invested in their own development. If they are not invested, it is not inequitable to decline to invest time and money in their development. Moreover, talent must be considered contextually. For example, to be considered a talented mathematician involves different skills from those required to be talented in one of the many fields where an outgoing personality and good people skills are part of the job. (Bob Zimmer, the late president of the University of Chicago, was one of those rare individuals with talents that would qualify him for the elite in just about any context—among other things, he was a world-class mathematician, an inspiring leader, a strong advocate for freedom of expression, and a superb fundraiser. One of his favorite jokes was that you could tell a mathematician was an extrovert if he or she stared at *your* shoes.) We must wean ourselves from an excessive reliance on test scores, GPAs, and credentials as definitive evidence of talent.

Effort—This surely belongs in the definition, but we need to recognize that a desire for a decent work-life balance is not evidence of a lack of energy. Effort, and the closely related subject called dedication, are not exclusively measurable by the number of hours spent at a task or at one's desk. Efficiency is a relevant consideration.

Integrity—Jefferson was correct! And only a person of high integrity can sincerely and convincingly convey that all-important "tone at the top." Moreover, when individuals in positions of "power and influence" do not have a moral compass that would prevent them from cutting corners during times of stress, such a shortcoming can damage their organization and cause physical and financial harm to others. Their improprieties can also lead to a loss of confidence in authority, even more than would occur from a good faith mistake in judgment. Warren Buffett, in describing who he wants to hire, said: "We look for intelligence, we look for initiative or energy, and we look for integrity. And if they don't have the latter, the first two will kill you, because if you're going to get someone without integrity, you want them lazy and dumb."[2]

Life experience—There are experiences outside the realm of education and fancy internships that can be invaluable in shaping and helping to predict the potential of an individual. In the context of college admissions, Justice Lewis Powell encouraged consideration of "qualities . . . likely to promote beneficial educational pluralism . . . [such as] exceptional personal talents, unique work or service experience, leadership potential, maturity, demonstrated compassion, a history of overcoming disadvantage, [and] ability to communicate with the poor . . ."[3] These life experiences can come from service in the military, participation in team sports, volunteer jobs, waiting on tables, growing up in the inner city or rural America, and so on. Because such life experiences can be available even to those of a lower socioeconomic status, when they are appropriately included in a definition of merit, the size and breadth of the pool of those considered for "positions of success, power, and influence" will be greatly increased. A caveat: Consideration of life experiences supplements, but does not replace, the need to critically consider talent and the other elements of merit. Assigning too high a priority to life experiences could be too easily attacked as creating a stealth double standard for assessing people. As will be discussed, the application of a double standard has serious negative consequences.

Humility—This is the antidote to condescension. Conveying a message that "I don't have all the ideas" is an attribute that is associated with a leader who is a good listener and is open-minded about accepting the ideas of others. All of this can encourage colleagues to innovate and share ideas. It contributes to collaboration and will facilitate a useful relationship with an organization's outside constituents. A humble leader acknowledges the role of luck in his or her success. Humility also increases the likelihood of success of the individual, because others will be more likely to want to see that individual succeed and will be supportive.

Selfless ambition—This involves being interested in the success of an organization and one's colleagues, and not just personal success, reputation, or compensation. It tempers internal competition and contributes to collegiality.

Resilience—Only those with an extremely sheltered (and lucky) life will not have to deal with disappointment and occasional failures. Virtually every organization will undergo periods of crisis. An individual who is not able to cope with that reality and stress can create problems if they are placed in positions of "power and influence."

Fundamental kindness, empathy, and respect for others—An individual displaying these attributes will be one whom others will want to see succeed. Those lacking these attributes are more likely to be the type of person who will want to take advantage of their position of power in personal interactions with subordinates.

The foregoing eight elements of a robust definition of merit represent a baseline. In addition to the contextual aspects of talent, the particular context of an organization may require some additional elements, especially in determining who is to be elevated to be a CEO or put in a similar position of leadership.

There is a difference between "merit" and "worth." Yuval Noah Harari had this to say about the latter: "Most Westerners today believe in individualism. They believe that every human being is an individual, whose worth does not depend on what other people think of him or her. Each of us has within ourselves a brilliant ray of light that gives meaning to our lives."[4] In contrast, meritocracy involves what "other people think." It operates by having others apply a definition of merit for purposes of deciding whether an individual should be "moved into positions of success, power, and influence."

DETERMINING MERIT

Applying an appropriate definition of merit to individuals requires diligence and self-awareness on the part of decision-makers.

Diligence is required to determine how well an individual comports with each of the elements of a definition of merit, with the goal of fairly assessing performance and future potential. A formal evaluation process has value. The solicitation of the views of a broad group of an employee's peers and their subordinates can be useful. Giving an employee an opportunity to respond to an assessment can provide additional information, provide the employee with a learning experience and also make the process feel more fair. Because, in the aggregate, assessments are highly subjective, self-awareness on the part of an assessor is critical.

Self-awareness starts with understanding and appreciating the notion of unconscious bias. Most leaders have heard about this issue in the context of race. It can be present along other lines as well, including gender. Take the example of assessing the effort and dedication of employees who are parents. Unfortunately, it is all too common that, when a man leaves work early to coach a child's soccer team, he is observed to be a great dad; when a woman does the same thing, bogus questions can be raised by some about her dedication to her career.

In addition to unconscious bias, there is the question of cognitive bias. The medical profession pays a lot of attention to this subject, because of how it can affect diagnoses and care. While there are many types of cognitive bias, some are particularly applicable to making hiring and promotional decisions. One form is "confirmation bias"—defined as "a tendency to seek out or interpret information that supports preexisting beliefs." So, if a decision-maker had a strong favorable first impression of an employee (maybe because of credentials, to be discussed), all subsequent data may be interpreted in a way that confirms that impression. Another form is "anchoring bias," in which a decision-maker is overly influenced by the known opinion of another when arriving at his or her own assessment of an employee. Then, there is the "halo effect," in which an overall impression—perhaps based on physical appearance or charisma—skews a disciplined consideration of all of the elements of a definition of merit. Finally, there can be a bias on the part of a decision-maker to over-credit attributes and prioritize elements of the definition of merit to mirror their views of themselves.[5]

Concerns about bias, and the current interest in artificial intelligence, have led to questions such as, "Can AI enhance meritocracy within the workplace?" (the title of a published article).[6] Put another way, can AI play the role of a blind audition? There are a couple of concerns about using AI to determine the merit of an individual. First, there can be bias in the AI itself; it is only as unbiased as the algorithm being applied. This is a matter of sufficient concern that various federal agencies have issued cautionary guidance on the subject (for example, the Joint Statement on Enforcement Efforts Against Discrimination and Bias in Automated Systems issued in 2023 by the Consumer Financial Protection Bureau, the Department of Justice, the Equal Employment Opportunity Commission, and the Federal Trade Commission).[7] Second, while an algorithm might be able to assess the presence or absence of some elements of a robust definition of merit, can it really assess, for example, elements such as humility, selfless ambition, and fundamental kindness? Thus, it seems unrealistic to rely to any substantial degree on AI for purposes of determining who belongs in the most significant roles in any organization.

TENURE

Most people think of "tenure" in terms of academia, although it is applicable to a greater or lesser extent in other organizational contexts. In academia, tenure is defined as "an indefinite appointment that may be terminated only for cause or under extraordinary circumstances such as financial exigency or of a bona fide department or program discontinuation."[8] It is justified in terms of assuring academic freedom and encouraging people to join the profession. Although advocates of tenure disagree, it is sometimes thought of as a guarantee of lifetime employment. Thus, tenure raises the issue of durability of merit. If a person meets standards embodied in the applicable definition of merit and is promoted to a position of "power and influence," but later his or her talents fade or become outdated, their efforts wane, their integrity is tested or there is some other erosion in meeting elements of the definition of merit, a well-functioning meritocracy should not allow them to be protected by tenure. But there can be a question of what degree of erosion would provide "adequate cause" for terminating someone with tenure. This concern may be part of the reason that some universities (and other organizations that adopt a version of tenure) have reduced the number of those on a "tenure track."[9]

A practice similar to tenure is seniority. In that practice, individuals can be given priority over others for selection to positions of authority, or even for purposes of compensation levels, solely because of longevity. It can clearly be anti-meritocratic.

MERITOCRATIC INHERITANCE

Jefferson's "artificial aristocracy [was] founded on wealth and birth."[10] When the wealthy have greater access to quality education, when their "networks" create employment opportunities for their children even despite shortcomings in their individual merit and when upward mobility is as a result not available to a deserving portion of the population, that is when a supposed meritocracy tilts toward an "artificial aristocracy" or "inherited meritocracy." In her speech at the 2024 Democratic National Convention, Michelle Obama referred to "the affirmative action of generational wealth."[11] As one observer put it, "inheritance" and "social and cultural capital" are non-merit factors that "suppress, or even negate, the effects of individual merit."[12]

Raj Chetty, a Harvard economist, and two colleagues published a paper in 2023 that illustrates meritocratic inheritance, the interrelationship between the two stages of meritocracy and credentialism. That paper might be summarized with a pithy phrase—"affluence begets affluence." As to the first stage—access to education—they note that "children from families in the top 1 percent are more than twice as likely to attend an Ivy-plus college . . . as those from middle-class families with comparable SAT/ACT scores." They attribute this to three factors: legacy admissions; "weight placed on non-academic credentials, which tend to be stronger for students applying from private high schools that have affluent student bodies"; and recruitment of athletes. These three factors (and especially legacy) are generally "non-merit." The impact of this access on the second stage is notable, according to the study—"attending an Ivy-plus college instead of the average highly selective public flagship institution increases students' chances of reaching the top 1 percent of the earnings distribution by 60 percent." The authors conclude that "highly selective private colleges . . . could diversify the socioeconomic backgrounds of America's leaders by changing their admissions practices," including by adopting a "need affirmative" policy.[13]

CREDENTIALISM

Credentialism is defined as "belief in or reliance on academic or other formal qualifications as the best measure of a person's intelligence or ability to do a particular job."[14] It has been described as "the last acceptable prejudice." Our society has been accused of "relentless credentialism."[15]

Academic credentialism takes two forms. First, there is the screening requirement of some employers for a diploma from a four-year college to be considered for a job, even when the actual position doesn't really require that level of education. (Reforms that push back on this form of credentialism are discussed in chapter 7. For the reasons mentioned there, however, high-potential youth should not be urged to settle for less than a four-year college diploma.) The second form is the excessive attention given to enrollment in elite educational institutions—starting with selective public high schools (e.g., Stuyvesant). The Ivy-plus colleges and the highly ranked professional schools are viewed as something of a holy grail. (Perhaps for good reason, according to Professor Chetty.) That can result in tremendous pressure on teenagers, sometimes from tiger moms (and dads) and sometimes by the kids themselves. This phenomenon has been described in a recent book by Jennifer Breheny Wallace entitled *Never Enough: When Achievement Culture Becomes Toxic.*[16] And parental pressure is humorously captured in a *New Yorker* cartoon in which a son is comforting his obviously distressed mother by saying "Don't cry, Mom. Lots of parents have children who didn't get into their first-choice college, and they [clearly, referring to the parents] went on to live happy, fulfilled lives."[17]

When the wealthy are able to game the system to help their children gain the credentials of degrees from high-prestige colleges and when those children can afford to take advantage of fancy uncompensated internships to dress up their résumés, then opportunities for jobs and advancement through meritocracy are less available to others.

An antidote: Employers should more fully credit other life experiences. For example, blue-collar job experiences or a stint in the military should be considered valuable credentials. Those experiences can be a source of empathy, humility, and common sense. David Novak, the retired CEO of Yum! Brands, grew up largely in trailer parks, went to the University of Missouri (the first in his family to go to college) and worked nights at a Holiday Inn. In a *Wall Street Journal* interview it was reported that he says "that his own humble background has helped him see the potential in others," an important skill for a leader.[18] There is one life experience that has even become a "badge of honor for business leaders who want to be viewed as humble and relatable"—working in a fast-food restaurant. It is amusing, but not surprising, to think of working at a McDonald's during one's youth as a credential![19]

The risk of using an emphasis on life experiences to mask a double standard in hiring, and the importance of rejecting the use of a double standard, were noted in this chapter and are discussed further in chapter 3. Other antidotes to credentialism that are being used by employers are discussed in chapter 7.

Credentialism can also be self-imposed by adults who obsess over their career advancement and titles. Concerns on the part of some job candidates that their academic credentials are lackluster can lead to embellishment (or worse) in résumés and on employment applications. If the individual is hired, those misstatements are typically not corrected and can carry forward during the course of a career and even in SEC filings. They are sometimes discovered during more rigorous vetting at the time the employee is being considered for a top job—even the CEO position—and can have devastating consequences for a career.

Interestingly, however, my recent survey of the undergraduate alma maters of the CEOs of the S&P 100 revealed that only eleven of them graduated from a so-called Ivy-plus college. About the same number went to Big Ten universities. Other schools listed include Rose-Hulman Institute of Technology, New Hampshire Technical College, Kettering University (f.k.a. the General Motors Institute), and Glendale Community College. (That said, a number of the CEOs who did not go to Ivy-plus colleges went on to get an MBA from one of the top five business schools.) Similarly, a recent academic study reported that the Ivy-plus colleges "account for more than 10 percent of Fortune 500 CEOs." Put another way, nearly 90 percent of the S&P 100 and Fortune 500 CEOs did *not* attend the Ivy plus![20]

A much more extensive survey of alma maters of the elite—business executives, high-level elected officials, MacArthur Foundation "genius grant" recipients, Pulitzer Prize winners, and Fulbright and Rhodes Scholars—is reported on in a book by *New York Times* columnist Frank Bruni. These surveys validate the name given to Bruni's book—*Where You Go Is Not Who You'll Be*.[21]

And while the credential of a degree from an Ivy League university might be assumed to be the ticket to great success as an entrepreneur, "a team at Stanford found that startup founders linked to the University of Cincinnati and the University of Utah . . . are more likely than Ivy League universities to produce a unicorn [a startup with a billion-dollar valuation]."[22]

There is a curious (even, amusing) development of anti-credentialism on the part of some politicians who effectively disavow sterling credentials in a populist appeal to those potential voters who have shown a disdain for the elite. As Pamela Paul, writing in *The New York Times*, explained "Republican politicians saddled with inconvenient Ivy League degrees [are put] in an awkward position, like the guy who shows up in a tux for a rodeo wedding."[23]

CULTURE WARS

We live in a time of culture wars. The term became most prominent in the US in 1991 with the publication by James Davison Hunter of his book *Culture Wars: The Struggle to Define America*.[24] Hunter's extended subtitle was "making sense of the battles over the family, art, education, law, and politics." The actual battles have raged most vigorously since the mid to late 2010s and now cover a broader range of issues than those identified by Hunter thirty years ago. Current issues in the culture wars include abortion (one of the original subjects identified by Hunter), gun control, what gets taught at schools (especially with respect to sexuality and to race, including critical race theory and the 1619 Project), LGBTQ (including pronouns and support of Pride Month), masculinity, immigration, climate change, and affirmative action and DEI programs. The ferocity of the current battles is exacerbated by disinformation in social media.

Hunter's observations from 1991 still ring true—"culture war emerges over fundamentally different conceptions of moral authority, over different ideas and beliefs about truth, the good, obligation to one another, the nature of community, and so on." As a result, "cleavages run much deeper" than simply politics.[25] Nevertheless, politicians have latched onto the culture wars as part of their fundraising and vote-getting pitches. And a favorite shorthand attack is an accusation of "wokeness." Much like the word "meritocracy," the meaning and use of the term "woke" has been turned on its head. Originally, it was a caution to Black folks to stay alert to discrimination.

In its use by politicians and others on the right, the term "bespeaks 'political correctness' gone awry."[26] Progressive acts by corporate America are labeled "woke capitalism." In an op-ed piece in *The Wall Street Journal* about his tussle with Disney, Governor Ron DeSantis wrote about "how the Left has pressured big companies like Disney to use their power to advance the woke political agenda." He went on to say that "the regrettable upshot of the woke ascendancy is that publicly traded corporations have become combatants over American politics and culture, almost invariably siding with leftist causes."[27] If by "leftist causes," he meant things like diversity and inclusion, he's probably correct. The term, of course, has a much broader connotation and includes supporting unions and socialism, concepts that most business leaders cannot be properly accused of siding with . . . invariably or ever!

Another politician has invoked the notion of meritocracy in the culture war battle over immigration—ironically, in support of exclusion rather than inclusion. Vivek Ramaswamy argues, "We must restore merit for who gets into America . . . eliminating lottery-based immigration in favor of meritocratic admission. Full stop."[28] Of course, Ramaswamy's parents met this standard; they were born in India and emigrated with engineering (father) and medical (mother) degrees.

UPWARD MOBILITY

A dictionary definition of upward mobility is "the capacity or facility for rising to a higher social or economic position."[29] A higher position than what? A practical standard might be to be better off financially than one's parents and that is certainly the goal for the disadvantaged portion of the population and, maybe even, for children of the working class. For children of middle-class and affluent families, focusing exclusively on financial measures is too narrow. They can realistically achieve a position of greater power and influence than their parents even if they do not enjoy higher incomes. And it has been reported that children born in 1980 have only a 50 percent chance of making more money than their parents (compared to a 92 percent chance for the boomer generation.)[30] Regardless, the potential for achieving upward mobility is "central to our country's narrative" and is "at the core of America's self-image."[31] A well-functioning meritocracy (that is, one that addresses the identified flaws, especially inclusiveness) provides equal opportunity for upward mobility to those who merit it.

A 2024 study from Harvard concluded that for individuals in "the 1978 and 1992 birth cohorts," (1) "household incomes in adulthood fell sharply for white children growing up in low-income families . . . [but] increased for white children growing up in high-income families"; and (2) "increased across all parental levels for Black children."[32] This suggests that class, rather than race, is playing the greater a role in determining upward economic mobility. This conclusion provides support for the notion of utilizing socioeconomic considerations in affirmative action programs—a notion that may now be legally mandated in any event. For individuals of all races who come from economically disadvantaged backgrounds, upward mobility often begins with financial aid that enables attendance at and graduation from college. The principal path to upward mobility after formal education is success within one's chosen field as part of an existing organization.

Another highly rewarding, but less common, path is successful entrepreneurship. As Bernie Marcus, a cofounder of Home Depot, put it, "My experiences led me to believe that preserving and expanding entrepreneurship is the key to advancing racial and economic equality. Entrepreneurship offers all Americans, no matter their background, a way to achieve financial independence and the American Dream."[33]

A successful entrepreneur exhibits many of the attributes included in a broad definition of merit. Success as an entrepreneur typically also requires creativity and grit (that is, persistence and resilience)—perhaps more than is needed to succeed in an existing organization.

Entrepreneurs frequently need financing to bring their ideas to fruition. Interestingly, funding sources do not seem to succumb to credentialism. For example, virtually none of the individuals who are included in lists of the most successful recent entrepreneurs graduated from any of the Ivy-plus universities. Oprah Winfrey graduated from Tennessee State, Sam Walton graduated from Mizzou, Steve Jobs dropped out of Reed, and the three founders of Home Depot graduated from Rutgers, Babson Institute, and Bucknell. Bill Gates and Mark Zuckerberg attended Harvard, but did not graduate. The exceptions were Chuck Schwab (Stanford) and Jeff Bezos (Princeton).

Those funding sources have typically been less supportive of Black entrepreneurs, especially Black women.[34] A fund called Fearless Fund has sought to remediate this situation by making grants to startups owned by Black women, using a contest offering "four winners $20,000 apiece and digital tools to assist business growth, as well as mentorship." But that approach was caught up in the post–Harvard/UNC litigation (discussed in chapter 3) and was enjoined by the US Court of Appeals for the Eleventh Circuit.[35]

As will be discussed, government has a role to play in fostering entrepreneurism. How that role is played out will be impacted by the post–Harvard/UNC litigation, as well as political considerations.

3

ELEMENTS OF MEANINGFUL REFORM

Clearly, the most controversial issue associated with reforming meritocracy is affirmative action. To some, affirmative action represents an exception to the application of meritocracy. To others (including me), affirmative action advances meritocracy by addressing continued limits on inclusion—which represent a major flaw in the current operation of our meritocracy—and by enhancing equal opportunity. Thus, if done right (that is, without using a double standard) affirmative action is perfectly consistent with meritocracy. This is a complicated subject, however, and a thoughtful consideration of affirmative action requires a good bit of context—involving an understanding of its history, goals, and recent legal constraints.

EQUALITY / EQUITY / EQUAL OPPORTUNITY

There is a great deal of controversy about, and some confusion as to the meaning of, these three concepts. For example, some critics of DEI programs confuse "equity" (the E in DEI) with "equality." So there is some benefit to providing some definitional precision and a discussion of how these concepts interrelate.

Equality connotes identical (or, at least, substantially similar) outcomes, regardless of abilities and maybe even effort. Equity "considers the specific needs or circumstances of a person or group and provides the types of resources needed to be successful."[1] Equal opportunity means giving folks a fair shot at equality, sometimes with the benefit of equity (i.e., a differential level of support), but with no guarantee of equality.

Equality is not the goal of meritocracy. Nor should it be. It is not a realistic goal. Moreover, as Yuval Noah Harari has observed, "people throughout the world have gradually come to see both social equality and individual freedom as fundamental values. Yet the two values contradict each other. Equality can be ensured only by curtailing the freedoms of those who are better off."[2] This may be one of the reasons that "in most versions of modern meritocracy . . . the selected objectives tend to be almost exclusively oriented toward aggregate achievements (without any preference against inequality)."[3]

A major goal of reforming meritocracy is to enhance equality of opportunity. This will increase "aggregate achievements" by putting the most meritorious individuals in positions of power and influence. It also reflects fundamental fairness. In addition, in the view of Fareed Zakaria, equal opportunity enables the "exercise [of] one's liberty."[4] Even equal opportunity can be a charged notion, however, because "studies demonstrate that advantaged group members misperceive equality as necessarily harming their access to resources and inequality as necessarily benefiting them" and "people often perceive situations to be zero-sum, even in situations that are not."[5] And there may be a sense of unfairness when others' opportunities are enhanced by equity—i.e., a different level of support.

One way to temper an adverse reaction to the concept of different levels of support in the name of providing equality of opportunity is to engage in a thought experiment involving a physical issue, rather than race or gender. Even if it weren't required as a "reasonable accommodation" under the Americans with Disabilities Act, very few would object to a school investing in wheelchair ramps for mobility challenged students or technology to help students with hearing or vision loss.

There might not even be a strong adverse reaction to spending taxpayer money for special tutoring for underprivileged students to help them qualify for Advanced Placement courses in order to help them with college admissions by addressing deficiencies in their substandard public schools. In contrast, if AP classes are canceled for all students in the name of equalizing opportunity, adverse reactions from parents of a privileged group will be quite strong and understandable. Equal opportunity should be achieved by elevating access to opportunity for the disadvantaged, not by eliminating opportunities for the privileged.

Nevertheless, some school districts are experimenting with eliminating "gifted student" programs in primary and middle school grades, in part to eliminate internal racial segregation within otherwise diverse student populations. And as of May 2024, there was pending litigation challenging the gifted students programs in the New York City public schools as causing "systemic exclusion" of Black and Latino students[6] There is some evidence that the education of high-achieving students is not harmed by eliminating such programs.[7] Other districts are experimenting with teaching high school freshmen together, regardless of achievement level (that is, delaying the implementation of "honors" programs). Some districts "report mixed success in widening the pool for advanced classes" after freshman year, but students who otherwise would have had freshman honors classes apparently still had success in national exams.[8]

RACIAL DISCRIMINATION

The role of racial discrimination is one of the central issues in any analysis of inadequate inclusiveness in the current version of meritocracy, and the availability of equal opportunity.

At a societal level, discrimination can be argued to be attributable to *ongoing* systemic racism. Current-day consent decrees involving police departments in various cities and the felt need of Black parents to give their sons "the talk" about how to behave during a traffic stop are regrettable evidence in support of this assertion. As are the racially motivated redistricting efforts that have been found to be violations of the Voting Rights Act of 1965 and the efforts to suppress voting by Black citizens. Systemic racism has been argued to result in a "serious US public health problem."[9] It is also thought to be one of the causes of racial disparities in life expectancy.[10] And it is noteworthy that the maternal mortality rate for Black people is 2.6 times the rate for white people, and that "Black women have a 53 percent increased risk of dying in the hospital during childbirth, no matter their income level, type of insurance, or other social determinants of health, suggesting systemic racism seriously impacts maternal health."[11]

Moreover, Michelle Alexander makes a pretty compelling case that the war on drugs in the 1980s and 1990s amounted to systemic racism. In her best-selling 2010 book *The New Jim Crow*, she asserts that there was disparate treatment of nonviolent drug offenders based on race. For example, in her preface to the tenth anniversary edition, she states that "Black people charged with possession of crack in the inner cities were still punished far more harshly than white people in possession of powder cocaine in the suburbs."[12] This led to mass incarceration of a significant portion of nonviolent offenders in the Black community and ongoing adverse impacts of incarceration that continue well beyond the release of a prisoner.

Perhaps another way of expressing the notion of persistent systemic racism is "caste." In her best-selling book entitled *Caste*, Isabel Wilkerson defines caste as "the powerful infrastructure that holds each group in its place." She states further that "race in the United States is the visible agent of the unseen force of caste" and that we have a "race-based caste pyramid in the United States."[13]

In the alternative, it can be argued that as a country, we are dealing with the lingering effects of *prior* systemic racism. Just one example of the need to do this is the Community Reinvestment Act of 1977, a "seminal piece of legislation intended to address inequities in access to credit . . . including race-based redlining."[14] "Redlining" is a term that refers to maps issued by the federal government in the 1930s that delineated areas of a city in which homeowners would not qualify for bank loans backed by government insurance. Those areas were largely Black neighborhoods. Redlining was systemic racism. And, as Richard Rothstein discusses at length in *The Color of Law*, redlining was only one form of "racially explicit government policies" that created residential segregation. He states further that, "although most of these policies are now off the books, they have never been remedied and their effects endure."[15]

At the level of individuals, there can be assertions of blatant racism (clearly true of white supremacists) or unconscious bias (on the part of many others).

Incidentally, for purposes of completeness, it should be noted that the Civil Rights Division of the Department of Justice once would pursue a case under Title VI of the Civil Rights Act of 1964 on the basis of "disparate impact"—that is, "practices having a discriminatory effect on protected groups, even if the actions or practices are not intentionally discriminatory." This is to ensure that "programs accepting federal money are not administered in a way that perpetuates the repercussions of past discrimination."[16] As might be expected, this concept was not without controversy or criticism.[17] Indeed, in May 2025, the Trump Department of Justice began the process for eliminating actions based upon disparate impact.

Assuming that there is an element of racial discrimination negatively impacting inclusiveness to some degree—frankly, a difficult thesis to dispute—it is unnecessary to decide whether the cause is ongoing systemic racism, the lingering effects of prior systemic racism, or racism at the level of individuals, just as it is unnecessary to assign weights to the various possible causes for purposes of thinking about reforming meritocracy.

Rather, the important question is what to do about it. One area of debate is whether the proper antidote is to pursue an agenda that is non-racist (essentially a passive approach) or anti-racist (more of an active approach). An anti-racist approach is embodied in affirmative action and DEI programs and policies, areas of controversy that are discussed later in this chapter. (By the way, as used herein, the term "anti-racist" refers to what John McWhorter called "second wave anti-racism"—"battling racist attitudes and [teaching] America that being racist is a moral flaw." It does not adopt the more extreme "third wave anti-racism," which he criticizes in his book *Woke Racism*.)[18]

Before turning to the approaches for addressing racial discrimination, a word about gender discrimination. It may be the case that significant progress has been made in addressing gender discrimination, but so long as it persists in any form (including sexual harassment), it is as damaging to a fully functioning meritocracy as racial discrimination. And a recent study by McKinsey and LeanIn.Org concluded that while "women hold more of the top jobs in companies than ever before . . . they lag behind men on crucial early promotions into management."[19] Finally, it is not for nothing that the terms "glass ceiling" and "glass cliff" are in the lexicon of business. So, the following discussion about increasing inclusion through affirmative action and DEI programs is applicable to both racial and gender discrimination.

AFFIRMATIVE ACTION

Affirmative action is a vehicle for reforming meritocracy by making it more inclusive. So long as it doesn't involve applying a double standard, it is not anti-merit. Nevertheless, affirmative action is the single most contentious issue associated with reforming meritocracy and (along with DEI programs) is the principal source of entanglement of meritocracy in the culture wars. Regrettably, the politicians on the two sides of the issue "do not talk to one another and have no electoral, social, or organizational incentive to do so."[20]

Affirmative action has been around for more than a half century, but is now receiving more attention than ever before. It is defined as "the use of policies, legislation, programs, and procedures to improve the educational or employment opportunities of certain demographic groups . . . as a remedy to the effects of long-standing discrimination."[21] Affirmative action is not about equality, but rather is about equal opportunity effected in part through equity. Affirmative action has both policy and legal (significantly, constitutional law) aspects. In both aspects, the question is this: What is *now* the proper purpose of affirmative action? Is it to remediate the lingering effects of systemic racism against Black Americans, or is it to provide the benefits of diversity for all individuals who, regardless of race, participate in an academic, business, or other setting? Then there is the question—again relevant to both the policy and the legal aspects—of whether the "demographic groups" to benefit from enhanced opportunities should *now* be defined by race or by socioeconomic class.

The first use of the term is usually attributed to President Kennedy in his 1961 Executive Order 10925 requiring government contractors to "take affirmative action to ensure that applicants are employed, and that employees are treated during their employment, without regard to their race."[22] This articulation seems to strike a "non-racist," rather than an "anti-racist," posture.

The *policy justification* for affirmative action with more of an anti-racist approach was articulated by President Lyndon Johnson in 1965 in his commencement address at Howard University as follows—"You do not take a person who has been hobbled by chains and liberate him, bring him up to the starting line of a race, and then say 'You are free to compete with all the others,' and still justly believe that you have been completely fair.'"[23] (While "hobbled by chains" was a bit of hyperbole some 100 years after Emancipation, there was plenty of hobbling done by Jim Crow laws, disparities in educational spending, real estate redlining, and otherwise.) Johnson continued, "We seek . . . not just equality as a right and theory but equality as a fact and as a result."[24] Notwithstanding that bold pronouncement, his Executive Order 11246 went no further than prohibiting discrimination and requiring "affirmative action to ensure" treatment of employees and candidates for employment without discrimination. Similarly, Richard Nixon, in his Executive Order 11478, declared, "It is the policy of the United States to provide equal opportunity . . . [and] to prohibit discrimination . . . [and] to promote the full realization of equal employment opportunity through a continuing affirmative action program. . . ." In short, these executive orders provided for what Melvin Urofsky, in his extensive history of affirmative action, has labeled "soft" affirmative action ("doing away with barriers") rather than "hard" affirmative action (involving quotas).[25]

Those who oppose affirmative action on policy grounds make four principal arguments.

First, it has been nearly sixty years since that LBJ speech, and a lot has changed since then. Indeed, when the US Supreme Court validated affirmative action in law school admissions in 2003, Justice Sandra Day O'Connor wrote in her majority opinion that "race-conscious admissions policies must be limited in time" and that the "Court expects that twenty-five years from now [2028], the use of racial preferences will no longer be necessary to further the interest approved today."[26] The "interest approved" in 2003 was ensuring a "critical mass" of minority students. This notion of giving affirmative action an end date echoes the idea that it should be a "stopgap measure" as advocated in the 1991 book by Yale law professor Stephen Carter entitled *Reflections of an Affirmative Action Baby*.[27] This notion of an end date is in keeping with the hopeful (but ultimately naive) suggestion that, with the election of Barack Obama, we had entered a "post-racial" state of being "where race no longer matters and racial hierarchies were a thing of the past."[28]

Second, when affirmative action is used to advance one minority group, it can be operated to the detriment of both those in the majority and of other minority groups that excel. This is essentially the assertion of the plaintiffs in the Harvard/UNC admissions case. And this may have been a contributing factor to the failure of the Proposition 16 referendum in California in 2020. That proposition unsuccessfully sought to reverse a constitutional ban on affirmative action programs adopted in 1996 "in the operation of public employment, public education, and public contracting."[29]

Third, in the particular context of college admissions at highly selective universities, opponents of affirmative action (whether race-based or socioeconomically based) argue that it is the members of the middle class who are being disadvantaged. They argue that affirmative action benefits the lower class and that children of affluent parents already have a leg up in admissions to highly selective schools (a position that has considerable supporting data). Thus, it is the middle class that is being discriminated against; one cause of the "hollowing out" of the middle class.[30] The obsession with highly selective schools under-credits the educational and other benefits that can be realized by matriculating at less-selective schools, but against a backdrop of credentialism makes some sense.

The final argument made by those in opposition: Affirmative action inevitably involves the application of "double standards"—that is, applying lesser requirements to underrepresented minorities. It is, therefore, antithetical to meritocracy. As a result, it weakens organizations. It is argued that it leads to employing underperformers who cannot be fired out of fear of litigation. And for high performing minorities who did not need a lower standard, it detracts from their accomplishments. As Stephen Carter wrote, because he was a Black man in an elite setting, the mere possibility of a double standard meant that he wore a label reading "do not assume that this individual is qualified!"[31] In the context of admission to colleges, it has been asserted that "Racial preferences [presumably using a double standard] have tragically mismatched students with schools, funneling them into institutions where they were in over their heads, pooling at the bottom of the class academically, or dropping out."[32]

A motivation for arguments against affirmative action by some (but certainly not all who take that position) is similar to the motivation described for opposing equal opportunity—fear of lost opportunity or, as most emotionally phrased, fear of "replacement." Opposition to affirmative action may, in some cases, be attributed to racism. A possible solution is to expand the goals of affirmative action to *also* include providing opportunities to those living in rural communities or to also use disadvantaged socioeconomic status as a criteria. A group of universities (including a number of the Ivy-plus colleges) have created an initiative called the STARS College Network (the acronym stands for "small-town and rural students") designed to "help students from small-town and rural America enroll in, succeed at, and graduate from the undergraduate program of their choice."[33] The network anticipates providing $7.4 billion in financial aid and programs for targeted students over a ten-year period.[34] (The use of the word "also" in that earlier sentence should be emphasized. Using rural residency or socioeconomic status, as an alternative to race, rather than as a supplement, would abandon the notion that a purpose of affirmative action is to remediate the ongoing impact of historic systemic racism, but that may now be legally required.)

Those who support affirmative action emphasize the benefits of diversity in any organization, educational or business. Those benefits include an enrichment of the cultural experience and negating the risk of groupthink that can be caused by homogeneous experience and that can impede thoughtful decision-making. Businesses (including those that filed amici briefs in the Harvard/UNC cases) support affirmative action in university admissions because they are seeking a diverse set of well-educated employees. They also recognize that being educated among a diverse cohort will better prepare any future employee to live and work in a pluralist society. Businesses with global operations and customers also understand that being represented by a largely white group of executives and workforce could put them at a competitive disadvantage.

Other supporters of affirmative action rely most heavily on a need to remedy the lingering effects of systemic racism. They argue that not enough has changed since LBJ's speech. This is evidenced by continuing racial disparities in income and wealth, healthcare (including maternal mortality), quality public education and so on. A 2017 study investigating "change over time in the level of hiring discrimination in US labor markets" concluded "We observe no change in the level of hiring discrimination against African Americans over the past twenty-five years."[35] And a 2023 study about "occupational segregation between Black and white workers in the US labor force" (namely, the exclusion of Black workers from "more desirable high-status jobs") concludes that "considerable racial occupational segregation . . . persists today regardless of educational attainment" with "significant consequences for wage inequality."[36]

Many of the strongest supporters of diversity agree with an element in one of the arguments against affirmative action. For all the reasons given, they oppose achieving diversity by application of a "double standard." A double standard is tokenism on steroids, and it feeds impostor syndrome.

It is possible to have a program of affirmative action and achieve diversity without applying a double standard. In some instances, this requires making an investment in building a pipeline of individuals with appropriate skills and education in order to increase the pool of available talent. Examples of pipeline programs—including "internal" pipelines—are discussed in chapters 6 and 7. Regardless of the size of the pool, employers need to utilize the robust definition of merit described in chapter 2. One of the biggest challenges, especially in hiring for entry-level positions, is resisting the temptation to succumb to credentialism as a proxy for talent. Another challenge has already been noted. As important as life experience can be as an element of merit, it cannot be used (or appear to be used) to create a stealth double standard.

So, how does an employer decide between one candidate with superior academic credentials (say a magna graduate from an Ivy-plus college) and another candidate with an adequate but lesser academic record but who, in the words already quoted from Justice Powell, has "a history of overcoming disadvantage"? The answer may well be "it depends." What is the job or position being filled? In the specific context, is one profile more predictive of future success than the other? How do the candidates compare along the lines of the other elements of a definition of merit? The answers to these questions may tilt in favor of one candidate over the other. However, if the outcome of balancing these considerations is, in essence, a tie, then give priority to the candidate who will help achieve diversity. A caveat: Given the aggressiveness of the anti-diversity activists, it is not out of the question that they would challenge this kind of "tie goes to the runner" approach, if the "runner" were to be defined exclusively along racial lines. (By the way, it is entirely possible that the magna grad in this hypothetical is from a wealthy family in a minority group and the other candidate is a white man from rural Appalachia!)

None of this is to suggest that avoiding a double standard is easy. And sometimes it can be difficult to convince colleagues within an organization that it is adhering to a single standard—especially if decision-makers are perceived to have personal financial incentives to "make the numbers."

The *legal component* of the affirmative action debate starts with the Equal Protection Clause of the Fourteenth Amendment of the US Constitution. That clause, part of the Amendment proposed and ratified in the immediate post–Civil War period, provides that "no state shall . . . deny to any person within its jurisdiction the equal protection of the laws." It applies to "state actors" as well as states and prohibits racial discrimination. In 2023, in the long-awaited decision in the Harvard/UNC admissions case,[37] the US Supreme Court effectively "gutted" (the word used in both the *New York Times* and *Wall Street Journal* headlines) the use of race-based affirmative action in college admissions.

While a full explication of the Supreme Court's reasoning is beyond the scope of this book (and perhaps the patience level of the target audience), some of the key points should be understood for two reasons. First, that understanding will help leaders of the private sector anticipate the implications of the decision for the efforts they are undertaking to foster diversity in their own organizations. Second, as discussed in chapter 8, many of those leaders have a role to play as trustees or donors to universities.

The key points made by Chief Justice John Roberts in presenting the opinion on behalf of the six-three majority start with the statements that "racial discrimination in public education is unconstitutional" and that "the Constitution's pledge of racial equality" is applied in a variety of contexts. He then notes that, to be allowed, any exception to equal protection must "survive a daunting two-step examination known in our cases as 'strict scrutiny.'" Step one: "whether the racial classification is used to 'further compelling governmental interests.'" Step two: "whether the government's use of race is 'narrowly tailored'—meaning 'necessary'—to achieve that interest."

The chief justice rejected the rationale articulated by LBJ in 1965, noting that "remedying . . . the effects of 'societal discrimination'" has not been found to be a compelling justification for purposes of satisfying strict scrutiny. In contrast, in their compelling book published just before the decision in Harvard/UNC, Lee Bollinger and Geoffrey Stone (two preeminent constitutional scholars who were formerly a president and a provost, respectfully, of Ivy-plus universities) argue that affirmative action in college admissions should be about "America's duty to correct the injustices that have been inflicted, uniquely, on Black Americans and inhibited their opportunity to develop and express their full talents."[38]

On the other hand, according to the chief justice, "obtaining the educational benefits that flow from a racially diverse student body" is a "constitutionally permissible goal." It certainly should be, given the benefits described by the US Departments of Justice and Education: "Research has shown that [racial and ethnic] diversity leads to, among other things, livelier and more informative classroom discussions, breakdown of prejudices and increased cross-racial understanding, and heightened cognitive development and problem-solving skills" and that "the benefits of diversity in educational institutions extend beyond the classroom . . . [by making students] better prepared for our increasingly racially and ethnically diverse society and the global economy."[39]

Despite these benefits, there are limits to what can be done legally to achieve them—no quota system could be used; there could be no "multitrack program with a prescribed number of seats set aside for each identifiable category." A third limitation seems to be what made the biggest difference in the recent cases—"The role of race had to be cabined. It could operate only as 'a plus' in a particular applicant's file." A later quotation from the majority opinion supports the notion that this third limitation may have been what carried the day—"College admissions are zero-sum. A benefit provided to some applicants but not to others necessarily advantages the former group at the expense of the latter." That observation followed a recitation of a finding by the court below that "Harvard's consideration of race has led to an 11.1 percent decrease in the number of Asian Americans admitted to Harvard."

Three other aspects of the opinion bear mention. First, by way of a footnote, the Court created what has been called the "military academy exception" to the application of the ban. This, despite the fact that a majority of the new officer corps comes from ROTC programs (such as those at Harvard) and not the academies. The same group that sued Harvard filed suit in three different federal judicial circuits against the Army, Air Force, and Naval Academies, testing the Court's footnoted exception. As of early 2025, the cases were at various stages of litigation—with the district court judge in the Naval Academy case ruling that its "race-conscious admissions policies withstand strict scrutiny because the Naval Academy established a compelling national security interest in having diverse officer corps . . . that represents the country it protects and the people it leads."[40] Nevertheless, in January 2025 the Trump Department of Defense mooted the military academy exception with a memo stating that there would be "no consideration for race, ethnicity or sex" in admissions to the service academies. Second, the Court rejected the notion that a university has an unlimited ability "as a matter of academic freedom 'to make its own judgments as to . . . selection of its student body.'" Finally, "nothing in this opinion should be construed as prohibiting universities from considering an applicant's discussion of how race affected his or her life," but the Court cautioned that "universities may not simply establish through application essays or other means the regime we hold unlawful today." In September 2023, the Department of Education weighed in with a report entitled *Strategies for Increasing Diversity and Opportunity in Higher Education*.[41] In that paper, the department provided guidance for how to respond to the Harvard/UNC decision. Among the strategies outlined were to "invest in targeted outreach and in pathways programs," placing "meaningful emphasis on student adversity, resiliency, and inspiration" in admissions decisions; "increasing affordability"; and cultivating "supportive environments and providing material support" programs.

While the full impact of the Harvard/UNC decision on undergraduate admissions remains to be seen, the first post-decision cycle of admissions provides a possible preview, although it has been observed that there is some murkiness in the data.[42] A number of highly selective colleges have reported rather sharp declines in the percentage of students who are Black in their entering classes for the fall of 2024—Amherst from 11 percent down to 3 percent; Brown from 15 percent to 9 percent; MIT from 15 percent to 5 percent; Harvard from 18 percent to 15 percent.[43] Especially when the entering class percentage drops to single digits, and in light of the fact that Black students who stay in school through graduation is a smaller number than those who started as freshmen, one is left to wonder whether the "critical mass" of minority students that Justice O'Connor referred to in her 2003 opinion is being achieved. Time will tell whether these percentages will rebound as a result of adopting the strategies described by the Department of Education or otherwise.

In the meantime, there are those who believe that this early data—and, in particular, the fact that the percentage of Asian American admittees has not gone up at some schools—is evidence that "some elite colleges dodge" the requirements of Harvard/UNC by "cheating."[44] And the group that filed that suit is foreshadowing playing the part of a private enforcer by threatening to investigate Princeton, Yale, and Duke because there were "notable declines in Asian American enrollment" in the fall of 2024.[45]

Another thought about "critical mass." Shouldn't it be judged on a school-by-school basis? That is, if a particular school's percentage of minority students—overall or in selected majors—for the duration of four years is below what its administration and board deem to be a critical mass for purposes of fulfilling its educational mission, shouldn't it be able to take reasonable steps to address that? In keeping with a rejection of the application of double standards, race and the achievement of diversity would be used only when selecting between equally qualified candidates. The Supreme Court may have opened the door to this approach with its footnote about the military academies, although this concept may have already been proposed to the Court in the brief filed by UNC, and rejected.[46]

In addition to challenging affirmative action in undergraduate admissions, activists emboldened by the Harvard/UNC decision have set their sights on a federal program designed to encourage certain students seeking doctoral degrees in science and math.[47] The Ronald C. McNair Postbaccalaureate Achievement Program provides support for students in one of three categories: "a low-income individual who is a first-generation college student"; "a member of a group that is underrepresented in graduate education" (with Black people, among other minority groups, specified); a member of another group "that is underrepresented in certain academic disciplines." The program does not exclude white or Asian students (and they may qualify under the first category), but those students represent only about 20 percent of the program's recent beneficiaries.[48] In December 2024, a lawsuit filed in federal court to challenge the program was dismissed by the trial court judge on procedural grounds.[49]

While affirmative action based on race in college admissions was struck down in the Harvard/UNC decision and the McNair program is also being challenged, it remains to be seen if attempts that were immediately launched to give that decision broader application to businesses will succeed and what will be the response to socioeconomic based affirmative action. Some insight into that issue was provided shortly after the decision in Harvard/UNC by dueling letters issued by state attorneys general (AGs).

In a letter signed by thirteen Republican AGs and sent to the CEOs of the Fortune 100 companies, the Republican AGs stated that "companies that engage in racial discrimination should and will face serious legal consequences." As examples of racial discrimination, the letter cites "explicit racial quotas and preferences in hiring, recruiting, retention, promotion, and advancement," as well as "race-based contracting practices . . . providing overt preferential treatment to customers on the basis of race, and pressuring contractors to adopt the company's racially discriminatory quotas and preferences." At the very end of the letter, the AGs seem to support affirmative action based on socioeconomic considerations: "Social mobility is essential for the long-term viability of a democracy, and our leading institutions should continue to provide opportunities to underprivileged Americans."[50] In 2019, the US Department of Agriculture reported that "across all races and ethnicities, US poverty rates . . . were higher at 15.4 percent in nonmetro (rural) areas than in metro (urban) areas at 11.9 percent."[51] It is probably not a coincidence that the thirteen AGs who signed the letter were from states with significant rural populations, including six of the ten most rural states.

In contrast, the Democratic state AGs wrote, "While we agree with our colleagues that 'companies that engage in racial discrimination should and will face serious legal consequences,' we are focused on actual unlawful discrimination, not the baseless assertion that any attempts to address racial disparity are by their very nature unlawful." The letter went on to "condemn the [Republicans'] letter's tone of intimidation" and to "applaud the Fortune 100 for your collective efforts to address historic inequities, increase workplace diversity, and create inclusive environments."[52] Similarly, the US Equal Employment Opportunity Commission issued the following statement following the Harvard/UNC decision: "It remains lawful for employers to implement diversity, equity, inclusion, and accessibility programs that seek to ensure worker of all backgrounds are afforded equal opportunity in the workplace."[53] And consulting firms and business schools continue to promote DEI programs and services. (See appendix B.)

This difference of opinion will be resolved in the courts. As of August 2023, lawsuits challenging DEI programs had been filed by conservative groups against a number of companies (or their boards of directors), including Amazon, Starbucks, and Comcast. Interestingly, in claims against boards, one defense might be the business judgment rule. That rule essentially defers to decisions made by directors so long as they have exercised their fiduciary duties and the decision has any rational connection to long-term shareholder value. In the admissions cases, the universities tried an analogous approach—citing academic freedom—but that failed.

DEI PROGRAMS

If affirmative action brings diverse individuals through the door, diversity, equity, and inclusion programs are designed to help the population of an organization remain diverse, with the emphasis on "equity" and "inclusion." DEI programs have been attacked as "woke," "virtue signaling" and (as previously noted) discriminatory. There are reports that chief diversity officers are leaving companies and that diversity-focused employees are being laid off.[54] There are reports of companies stepping back from giving grants and providing other assistance to minority-owned small businesses.[55] In contrast, there are also reports that consumer goods companies are "reinforcing their commitment to those programs."[56] There is evidence that successfully pursuing diversity (an element of reform) is positive from a business standpoint. According to a 2015 study from McKinsey, "new research makes it increasingly clear that companies with more diverse workforces perform better financially." The study attributes this to more diverse companies' being "better able to win top talent and improve their customer orientation, employee satisfaction, and decision-making" and that those companies are likely to have "some level of competitive advantage."[57] Another observer has labeled diversity as "the mother of creativity."[58]

Even when affirmative action is implemented without a double standard, there may still be a need for providing a differing level of support (that is, equity) in order to level the playing field and give everyone an equal opportunity to succeed. For example, two equally educated and energetic individuals of good character may be joining an organization from very different backgrounds. One may be the third-generation member of his or her family to be employed in that type of organization; the other may be the first in the family. The former person will likely be more comfortable in the milieu and have access to family members who can provide coaching about what to expect and how to succeed. The latter might be totally at sea. The former may have members of his or her family who know individuals at a senior level within the organization, who will be expected to "look after" the new employee. The latter is unlikely to have the benefits of a network. Equity could involve giving the latter individual more attention and mentoring. Inclusion could involve having the mentor help seek out opportunities for growth and advancement for the latter individual.

Equity also involves fair treatment of those who make an organization more diverse without the application of a double standard. This can be a relatively simple matter of fair implementation of a compensation system. Or, fair treatment can be more complex, as shown by the situation described in the recent book entitled *The Exceptions*. In 1999, MIT admitted to discriminating against female science faculty members, not just on pay, but also on credit for scientific discovery and resources required to do their work.[59]

The cause of DEI programs has been regrettably damaged of late. First of all, corporate diversity efforts are often viewed as ineffective. In a 2019 study based on a survey by the National Opinion Research Center at the University of Chicago, the Center for Talent Innovation reported that less than half of all professionals—regardless of race or ethnicity—think their companies have effective diversity and inclusion efforts.[60] Second, DEI programs can (in the words of a pro-diversity consultant) place "an overemphasis on identity groups and [have] a tendency to reduce people to 'victim or villain' . . . [and] alienate everyone."[61] Third, there have been reports of universities, in an effort to bolster their DEI programs, requiring what are too easily labeled, and appropriately discredited, as "diversity loyalty oaths" of applicants for faculty positions. (In May 2024, MIT dropped this requirement, and in June 2024 the Faculty of Arts and Sciences at Harvard did the same.) This makes it all too easy for some who oppose or are skeptical of diversity efforts to argue (rant?) that "in contemporary higher education, diversity competes with intellectual authority, based on scholarly and scientific accomplishment."[62] Another commentator concluded that a university's DEI "apparatus . . . is . . . all too often an engine of censorship and extreme political bias."[63] One opinion piece in *The Wall Street Journal* went even further, with the hyperventilating headline "DEI at Law Schools Could Bring Down America"![64]

Perhaps the most preposterous attack on DEI is a complaint filed by activists with the Department of Health and Human Services challenging the Cleveland Clinic's program "to prevent strokes and other conditions among minority patients"—a program that was developed in recognition of the fact that "Black men and women are at least two times as likely as white Americans to die from strokes."[65] What's next—opposing the funding of research on sickle cell anemia?

Finally, there has been at least one instance in which an employer's diversity hiring efforts were alleged to be fraudulent. In a shareholder derivative suit and private securities litigation, it was alleged that Wells Fargo employees conducted "sham" interviews of diverse candidates to meet quotas and create a false impression that the bank was committed to DEI initiatives. The alleged behavior was also the subject of DOJ and SEC investigations (both of which were closed).[66]

The various forms of attack on DEI programs in corporate America, and companies' responses, are discussed in chapter 7.

The pushback on DEI programs has been so significant that, in July 2024, the SHRM (the Society for Human Resources Management, a 340,000-member "lobbying and advocacy group") created a new abbreviation—"I&D"—dropping the "E," which stood for equity.[67]

In their book *Tyranny of the Minority*, professors Levitsky and Ziblatt state that "multiracial democracy is hard to achieve."[68] Without efforts along the lines of DEI by whatever abbreviation it is known (in keeping with legal limitations on affirmative action and avoiding a double standard), it may be hard to achieve multiracial meritocracy.

IMPOSTOR SYNDROME

As noted in the discussion of affirmative action, achieving diversity through the application of a double standard has a number of downsides, including feeding "impostor syndrome." This concept was originally labeled the "impostor phenomenon" in a 1978 paper by two psychologists.[69] It is defined as "struggling with the sense that [a person hasn't] earned what they've achieved and are a fraud" resulting in a fear that "they're going to be 'found out.'"[70] This reaction can be particularly common among students who feel that they were admitted to a prestigious university only because of their race and among employees who feel that they were hired for the same reason.

One can speculate that it may also be experienced by students who believe they were admitted largely because of a preference given to "legacies," as well as employees who believe that they were hired primarily because of family connections. Impostor syndrome can cause students and employees to become depressed, or even quit, in reaction to the kind of setback in performance that just about anyone will experience at sometime during their academic or work careers. Impostor syndrome can deprive the individual of the resilience that is so important to success. The antidote is to explicitly state that the university or employer (as the case may be) does not apply a double standard—and for those institutions to make that statement true.

4

ROLE OF PHILANTHROPY

The subject of philanthropy is relevant to any consideration of meritocracy (and its reform) for a number of reasons. One of the outputs of meritocracy is the creation of an elite, whose members often enjoy significant financial reward. Because the elite will often have substantial financial resources, through philanthropy its members—individually and through the organizations they lead—have the ability to share their financial success. They can donate money (and their time) in ways that are targeted to ameliorate poverty and reduce income and wealth inequality and otherwise enhance equal opportunity. On the other hand, a good bit of philanthropy is not targeted in this way; worse, it is possible that some forms of philanthropy may actually exacerbate inequality and meritocratic inheritance if targeted in ways that benefit the already affluent.

This chapter will very briefly note the origins of philanthropy and then discuss both the various motivations that lead to philanthropy and the controversies related to philanthropy. How the private sector can utilize philanthropy as a tool for reforming meritocracy and revitalizing the American Dream will be discussed in part II.

ORIGINS AND MOTIVATIONS

The origins of philanthropy can be traced to the teachings of just about all religious faiths, including Judaism, Christianity, Islam, Buddhism, and Sikhism.[1] Or it can be based on a secular notion of noblesse oblige. Because philanthropy can have beneficial tax implications, modern philanthropy (and especially the creation of private foundations) has been argued to be state-subsidized.[2]

Some philanthropy is motivated by a desire to receive something in return—a quid pro quo. For example, the goal of a donation to a highly selective university might be to increase the chance for a child or grandchild to gain admission. Or the sought-after quid pro quo might be another example of the velvet rope economy—seeking to gain access to good seats at a university's athletic stadium or to ensure priority treatment at a hospital.

The motivation might be to further enhance the already positive reputation of an individual or an organization. As to the former, think of the number of university buildings, parts of buildings, and academic units named for prominent families and businesspeople. An example of the latter could be the 1998 donations by Sara Lee Corporation of its world-class collection of impressionist art to museums across the country. That could be viewed as an exercise in branding and marketing. At the time (before the explosion in art auction pricing), the collection was valued at about $100 million.

Other philanthropy might be motivated by the desire to rehabilitate a damaged reputation. This kind of giving—reputation "washing"—may be exemplified by the saga of Jeffrey Epstein and the gifts he made between his 2008 guilty plea and his 2019 arrest for similar sexual misconduct. Universities and not-for-profits need to be cautious about accepting gifts (especially those with naming rights) lest they find out too late that they are participating in reputation washing. One might speculate that reputation washing was part of the motivation behind Alfred Nobel's donation of his fortune for the establishment of the Nobel Prize—after all, his invention of dynamite resulted in his being labeled the "merchant of death."[3]

Still other philanthropy might be motivated by a desire to exercise control over the agenda or operations of an organization. That motivation may be manifested in the terms of a donor agreement.

But even beyond such terms, a major donor may feel entitled to exercise influence over the organization more generally. Consider, for example, the actions of large donors to the University of Pennsylvania and Harvard following the disastrous congressional testimony of the presidents of those institutions on the subject of free expression in the context of the Israeli–Hamas war.[4]

Some philanthropy is motivated by gratitude. Think of gifts to medical institutions following life-saving treatments received by a donor or compassionate care given to a late relative.

Perhaps the purest form of philanthropy seemingly has no element of self-interest because it is done anonymously. Consider the example of Chuck Feeney, the founder of Duty Free Shoppers Group. Through his foundation, and by the time of his death, he gave away more than $8 billion—virtually his entire self-made fortune. And it was reported that none of the many buildings constructed as a result of his gifts bear his name.[5] Another example is the anonymous donor whose $100 million gift started the Odyssey Scholarship Program at the University of Chicago to provide financial aid to undergraduates on the basis of need. (Amusingly, that donor is referred to as "Homer.")

Regardless of motivation, you would think that the significant amounts involved in, and societal benefits of, philanthropy would make it largely immune from controversy. As to amounts, consider this: In 2016, "Americans donated more than $390 billion to eligible nonprofit organizations" and 72 percent of that was from "living individuals." And "roughly 10 percent of the labor force" was employed by nonprofits.[6] So, between that and the religious origins, you might expect immunity from controversy. You would be wrong.

CONTROVERSIES

Issues with philanthropy have been raised by those writing about meritocracy, by those writing about philanthropy and even by those actively participating in philanthropy.

One author writing about meritocracy expressed her skepticism of philanthropy this way: "I do not advocate extending the noblesse oblige, or the altruistic philanthropy of the rich . . . the rich have plenty of ways through philanthrocapitalism [*sic*] to use donations to vastly extend their power and perpetuate new inequalities."[7] (I wonder what she thought of Chuck Feeney or whether she was even aware of him, given his well-cultivated low profile.) In contrast, another author embraces philanthropy and progressive taxation as "possible ways to reduce levels of inequality and restore more equity to the system," adding that "philanthropy, particularly that provided by the superwealthy, has the potential to promote meritocracy [by] . . . making it easier for those at the bottom of the system to reach the top . . . reducing the transfer of non-merit advantage across generations . . . and reducing non-merit disadvantage for those at the bottom of the system . . ."[8] A third author cautions that "we need to make sure that the [elite] . . . have much more of a sense of responsibility to the wider society."[9]

Then there are the views of those writing about philanthropy itself. Rob Reich, a Stanford University professor (and no relation to Robert Reich, the University of California, Berkeley professor and former secretary of labor in the Clinton administration), has written a provocative book with the subtitle "Why Philanthropy Is Failing Democracy and How It Can Do Better."[10] Professor Reich focuses heavily on the philanthropy of foundations, warning that "it can be a plutocratic exercise of power." (A similar theme is struck in another recent book entitled *The Bill Gates Problem: Reckoning with the Myth of the Good Billionaire* by Tim Schwab.) Professor Reich is particularly concerned with an absence of transparency and accountability on the part of foundations. He also argues that "philanthropy sits uneasily with equality," noting that it is "directed with surprising infrequency to the relief of poverty and assistance for the disadvantaged" and that "in some cases philanthropy actually produces or exacerbates inequality." He illustrates these points with a discussion of "local education foundations," or "LEFs." These organizations allow tax deductible contributions to public schools. Because LEFs exist largely in suburban areas, they actually expand the gap in per pupil spending between schools in affluent areas and those in the inner city. Using the concepts discussed earlier in this book, it might be said that LEFs facilitate meritocratic inheritance.

Those engaged in philanthropy don't always see things the same way. Those among the 236 signatories (as of 2022) to the "Giving Pledge" founded by Bill Gates and Warren Buffett have pledged to give away a majority of their wealth during their lifetime or at death. In contrast, an organization called Global Citizen launched a "Give While You Live" campaign. This notion of giving away wealth during one's lifetime is not a brand-new idea. In 1889, Andrew Carnegie published an essay entitled "The Gospel of Wealth." He was clearly an advocate for meritocracy (at least as practiced in his day). But he asked, "What is the proper mode of administering wealth after the laws upon which civilization is founded have thrown it into the hands of the few?" Of the three modes of administration that he identifies, he argues forcefully for disposing of "surplus wealth" during one's lifetime. And he labels leaving wealth solely to one's family as "injudicious" and not good for either the children of affluence or the state. The last of the three modes—"leaving wealth at death for public purposes"—risks that "the real object sought by the testator is not attained."[11]

Even large gifts made during a donor's lifetime can attract criticism. For example, the $300 million gift in 2023 from Ken Griffin to Harvard was criticized by the Left as a "wasteful" gift from one hedge fund to another (a reference to Harvard's $50 billion endowment).[12]

So, members of the elite who are interested in reforming meritocracy should consider how their philanthropy can be targeted to achieve that goal.

II

PRIVATE-SECTOR REFORMS

5

THE PRIVATE SECTOR LEADS THE WAY

One's perspective on whether efforts to reform meritocracy should be led by the governmental sector or the private sector is largely influenced by two considerations—a view as to what the goal of meritocracy should be; and an assessment of the competency and motivations of each sector.

Those who would put the reform in the hands of the governmental sector often seem to start with the view that the goal of a meritocratic society is not simply equal opportunity, but should be economic equality (or at least closing the income and wealth gap or reducing advantages enjoyed by the affluent). They recommend redistribution through tax policy—one author advocates a more progressive income tax and estate and gift tax reform;[1] another advocates a "progressive consumption tax."[2] Another argues that universities should lose their tax exempt status unless they draw half of their students from the bottom two-thirds of the income distribution.[3] A nontax policy suggestion has a decidedly Luddite tone—"promote middle-class labor by promoting ways of making goods and services that favor mid-skilled workers."[4] The most radical proposal echoes themes from Occupy Wall Street—"take the power away from the 1 percent and give it to the 99 percent," noting further that "the grossly inflated phenomenon of corporate power needs cutting down."[5]

The advocates for governmental action are also highly skeptical about relying on the private sector to reform meritocracy. This is a great example of attacks from both sides of the aisle. From the Left: "What is at stake is whether the reform of our common life is led by governments elected by and accountable to the people, or rather by wealthy elites claiming to know our best interests."[6] From the Right: "Woke capitalism" is "quietly wreaking havoc on American democracy" and leaving to "a small group of investors and CEOs [to] determine what's good for society rather than our democracy at large."[7]

A much more compelling case can be made that reform efforts should be led by the private sector—actions taken at the organizational level—market-based meritocracy. This is because the implementation of meritocracy during the post-education stage is most practically in the hands of leaders of private organizations. It is their organizations who employ approximately 85 percent of US workers. Thus, it is those leaders whose decisions about hiring, promoting, mentoring, and training have the broadest societal impact—far more than anyone in leadership at a governmental employer. And those leaders can also have an impact outside their own organizations, including on education.

Skepticism about the motivations of a majority of the elite is reflected in the questions: "Do you really trust the elite to reform the elite . . . to give up the opportunity to bestow meritocratic inheritance . . . to increase the competition to be faced by their own kids . . . to become humble?" Certainly, those whom I have observed closely over a legal career of nearly half a century are not categorically disqualified by selfish motives or otherwise from pursuing reform. I think many of the members of the elite want to see things get better for the disadvantaged members of society. This is derived from their sense of ethics, fairness, and (yes) noblesse oblige, or out of self-interest, or a combination of both.

Jim Crown provides a great example. He was the leader of a third generation of a family of dynastic wealth. He was also smart, hardworking, humble, and civic minded—attributes that he inherited from his father, Lester. Shortly before he died tragically in an accident, Jim initiated a gun violence prevention program in Chicago. In an interview at the time that program started, he illustrated the combination of motivations for philanthropy with this quote in the *Chicago Sun-Times*: "You've got altruism. But you've also got the enlightened self-interest of: I want to be safe, I want my workers to come to work, I want the tourists to patronize my business . . ."

Another source of skepticism is whether the elite can effect reform beyond the four walls of their organizations. It is a fair question whether the efforts of the private sector to do so would have more than success at the margins in addressing seemingly intractable societal problems. It is a fair question whether those in the private sector can be convinced to expend the time, energy, and even money to do so—especially if they feel that their efforts will not yield significant results. In short, isn't this a job for the government?

I am a lifelong centrist Democrat and generally believe that government can and should be helpful, but I have far more confidence in the private sector to get things done and create the equal opportunities that are at the core of meritocracy. This is not because I adhere to the view of Milton Friedman that "the free market would address racial inequities more effectively than governmental attempts."[8] Indeed, I point to the results of LBJ's Great Society programs in reducing the percentage of Americans living in poverty as evidence of what government can accomplish.[9]

Aside from efficacy, there are other reasons for favoring the private sector, including the need for stability of policy and a concern about how elected officials are currently elected and held accountable. Reforming meritocracy is a long-term, ongoing project. It is a journey, not a one-off project. Governmental administrations come and go—sometimes in a short period of time and with 180-degree shifts in policy. In addition, policy development often requires compromise by, or at least open-mindedness of, those on opposite sides of an issue. This is less likely when elements of what will be required to reform meritocracy are swept up in the culture wars. And we now live in a time when, as Peggy Noonan has put it, "lawmakers don't experience themselves as political figures doing the business of the nation but as actors in a streaming series called 'Populism!' on some tacky cable network. . . ."[10] In an article about the flood of members of Congress who are leaving in 2024, some of them who were interviewed for the piece "depicted an institution now dominated by brawlers and attention-seekers," with one describing their behavior as being "like they're all auditioning for a political reality show."[11]

There is another reason for not relying on government. Far too many in elective or appointive office seem to occupy those position for reasons other than merit. They are often people who would not succeed in corporate America. Indeed, there is a good argument that too many "safe seats" (in some ways a version of tenure) and effective (often single issue) demagoguery has led to an excess of mediocrity.

There is also a regrettable lack of good character on the part of too many elected officials. There are certainly many elected governmental officials in all branches of good—some, even, of impeccable—character. From the number of elected officials about whom that cannot be said, however, it appears that good character is not a priority consideration on the part of many in the electorate when deciding whom to support, financially and with votes.

It has not always been this way. In the 1970s, the career of Wilbur Mills, the powerful chairman of the House Ways and Means Committee was brought to an end by reports of his drunken dalliances with a burlesque performer. In the 1980s, Gary Hart, the front-runner for the Democratic presidential nomination dropped out of the race after reports surfaced of extramarital affairs. But since then, the careers of leading politicians of both parties—prominent examples being Bill Clinton (in the 1990s) and Donald Trump (most recently)—seem to have been unaffected by arguably even worse actions and reputations. And if those two had been public company CEOs, they would have been fired in a heartbeat! But we are living in what many observers have labeled the "post-shame era" of politics.[12]

Consider, also, how many elective officials you can think of who exemplify the element of merit labeled "selfless ambition." Compare the real-time reactions of some members of Congress to the events of January 6, 2021, with the subsequent positions taken by those same politicians. It appears that many of those people, on reflection, placed their highest priority on remaining in power. There were exceptions, to be sure—Mike Pence and Liz Cheney, among others—but far too few.

The toxic combination of safe seats, selfish ambition, and indifference by many voters (and even by members of Congress) to evidence of bad character on the part of candidates and incumbents and a broken campaign finance regime makes it challenging to have unalloyed confidence in government.

Based on the Edelman "trust surveys," I am not alone in having a higher regard for the private sector. In the 2023 survey, business was more trusted than government generally, CEOs were more trusted than government officials, business was thought to be a more reliable source of information than government, and businesses are thought to be far more competent and ethical than government.[13] Similarly, according to Pew Research Center, "public trust in government [is] near historic lows, with only 16 percent trusting the federal government to do 'what is right' either 'just about always' (1 percent) or 'most of the time' (15 percent)."[14]

That said, there is a role for government in all of this. Equal opportunity requires equality of certain things that are mostly in the exclusive province of government. Things like equal justice and equal voting rights. Government should address equal access to healthcare, environmentally safe neighborhoods and quality primary and secondary education.

Government can also smooth the road for entrepreneurs to achieve upward mobility by thoughtful application of regulations to startups. However, in the view of Bernie Marcus: "Unfortunately, government is moving in the wrong direction, erecting hurdles to entrepreneurship" with "regulations and taxes that disproportionately burden small businesses."[15]

Government should also administer a fair, efficient, and compassionate welfare system to address the needs of the poorest among us. In his book *Poverty, by America*, Matthew Desmond, a Princeton University sociologist, describes two major shortcomings in the current system. First, despite a significant increase in welfare spending, too many dollars are allocated to "activities that had little or nothing to do with reducing poverty." And second, "low-income Americans are not taking full advantage of government programs . . . [because] we've made it hard and confusing."[16]

As will be discussed in the next chapter, large professional services firms, out of necessity, have developed best practices designed to address many of the flaws of meritocracy as currently practiced. Those practices can be adopted and amplified by corporate America. Many companies have already done so. More should.

6

PROFESSIONAL SERVICES FIRMS HAVE SHOWN THE PATH FORWARD

Large, well-managed professional services firms—law firms, consultancies, auditors, financial service providers—have adopted best practices that have the effect of addressing flaws in meritocracy. Why is this? Because they really have no choice. The reputations of these firms are based on the merits of their professionals (individuals and teams), and can be sullied by the poor performance, lack of integrity, or elitist attitude of a very few. They must do meritocracy right!

Meritocracy is relevant to all aspects of managing talent and to the operations of a professional services firm. It is used as a pitch in recruiting. For example, McKinsey has stated that, as part of its goal to "create an unrivaled environment for exceptional people," it seeks to "sustain a caring meritocracy."[1] A fair application of meritocracy is critical for retention, especially at a time when the movement of professionals among firms is extremely common. Recruiting and promoting solely on the basis of merit is an element of risk management. "Lockstep" compensation based on seniority, once favored by many law firms, has given way to merit-based compensation using a broader set of criteria—including collaboration and collegiality—than simply "eat what you kill." (Compensating based solely, or even principally, on business generation, can lead to decidedly non-collegial behavior.) The notion that, once attaining partnership status, a lawyer is "tenured" gave way long ago. Meritocracy is a competitive necessity, critical in an era when relationships with firm clients must be continuously earned, and when high fee structures must be justified.

Before elaborating on some of the best practices that have been developed by law firms (the professional services firms I know best), let's pause on the "bad old days."

A HISTORY OF EXCLUSION

Some perspective on the dramatic increase in inclusion in the professional services firms is provided by a few vignettes about the legal profession in the immediate post-WWII period and even more recently.

- Sandra Day O'Connor graduated in 1952 from Stanford Law School. She was reportedly second or third in her class—just behind William Rehnquist. Upon graduation, the only job offer she received from a law firm was to work as a secretary. O'Connor and Rehnquist later reunited on the US Supreme Court.
- In 1956, Ruth Bader Ginsburg was one of nine female first year students (out of about five hundred) at Harvard Law School. It has been reported that then-Dean Erwin Griswold asked those women, "Why are you taking the place of a man?"[2] Nearly thirty years later, Griswold gave a speech in which he praised Ginsburg for her work on women's rights. (Interestingly, two of the most successful subsequent deans at Harvard Law were its first female dean, Elena Kagan, and Martha Minow, Kagan's successor.)
- In the early 1970s stories circulated about female law students being asked, in recruiting interviews, "Can you type?" The priceless response of one of those students was, "Yes and I can [expletive], too, but I don't do either for money."
- And as late as the 1970s, male partners in law firms would decline to staff women on their cases and transactions if those matters

would involve out-of-town travel, often denying women lawyers career-advancing assignments.

- Moreover, law firms were described to be predominantly either Jewish or Christian. A Stanford Law Review article entitled "The Rise and Fall of the WASP and Jewish Firms" stated "this was surprising because the large firm [in the "'golden era' of the 1950s and 1960s"] was purportedly a-religious and meritocratic."[3] In a 1976 article, a Wellesley College history professor put it this way: "Elite firms were as accessible and hospitable to non-whites, non-Protestants, and non-males as were medieval cathedrals to heretics."[4] While that is certainly hyperbole and many leading firms had Jewish partners (and even Jewish managing partners), it is also the case that many so-called white-shoe firms were not very diverse even into the 1970s.
- A 1987 article in the *Los Angeles Times* started with this observation: "A pattern of discrimination against Jews, Blacks, Latinos, and women marked the leading corporate law firms for most of their history."[5] No doubt the same observation would have applied to many of the leading firms in other major cities.

Clearly the earlier failures of inclusion described in these examples stilted the application of meritocracy. By limiting the supply of talent, they also represented tremendous lost opportunities for law firms.

ENHANCING INCLUSION

Those were the bad old days. Now law firms embrace practices that have enhanced inclusion and involve a new approach to recruiting, talent development and retention, addressing burnout, and unconscious bias.

Firms address "credentialism" (no small feat for a "learned profession") through a broader reach in recruiting. It has been decades since the elite firms have limited their interview schedules to the top ten law schools or focused most heavily on members of law reviews.

Firms understand that a reputation for credentialism can deprive themselves of excellent candidates. (Interestingly, the US Supreme Court seems to have remained heavily focused on credentials, or at least networks. According to a recent study, during a forty-year period ending in 2020, more than two-thirds of SCOTUS law clerks attended just five elite law schools.)[6]

In the recruiting process, firms are also crediting life experience (one of the elements of the robust definition of merit described in chapter 2). While service in the military, an interesting (and perhaps relevant) prior career, or "a history of overcoming disadvantage" (to quote Justice Powell) will not overcome a totally lackluster law school record, such factors can help a candidate differentiate himself or herself and lead to an offer of employment.

Importantly, thoughtful firms are aggressively resisting applying a double standard in hiring just to "make the numbers" in minority recruiting. In terms of self-interest, they recognize that minority attrition and a failure to advance minority associates to partner are more noticeable (and detrimental to morale and reputation) than having a smaller number in an entering class of associates. They also recognize the damage that can be done to individuals.

To address the fact that there are still too few minority students enrolled in law schools, some firms sponsor pipeline programs designed to encourage students at the college level (and even earlier) to consider going to law school. Those programs can also provide financial and other aid to facilitate the application process for those students—funding LSAT prep courses; acting somewhat like the private college counselors described in chapter 1; or running "boot camps" the summer before first year to give the students a bit of a head start.[7] And the American Bar Association (ABA) has offered its members a free program entitled "Best Practices for Legal Diversity Pipeline Programs."[8]

Incidentally, the legal profession clearly doesn't have a monopoly on pipeline programs. For example, in 2022, the American Institute of CPAs (AICPA) established its pipeline program called the Registered Apprenticeship for Finance Business Partners and announced its first corporate participants—Liberty Bank, Aon plc, and HP.[9] The program is "available to new hires and incumbent employers as well as those with four-year degrees and those earning two-year degrees."[10]

In addition to pipeline programs, a number of law firms provide "diversity scholarships" to students already in law school. These are provided to students who join a firm's summer program and should be viewed principally as a recruiting tool. Following the Harvard/UNC decision, such scholarships have also been attacked, and firms are adjusting their criteria for eligibility.

Firms recognize the benefit of investing in developing the talents of their lawyers. All new lawyers benefit from formal training programs that cover aspects of practice that are not taught in law schools (especially the elite schools). All benefit from mentoring, through both informal and formal programs. One innovative formal program involves "mentoring circles"—a group of associates meeting with a group of partners until natural connections are developed between an individual mentor and mentee. Some young lawyers, who come from backgrounds that do not include familiarity with the profession or the operations of an organization like a law firm, may require an enhanced level of support. (Recall the definition of "equity.") That enhanced support may include actions such as assigning mentors who are among the most senior partners in the firm and who may be more influential in helping mentees receive good assignments that will help them grow professionally.

Law firms lose lawyers whom they wish to keep for a variety of reasons. Women and minorities are increasingly being "poached" by law departments of clients and non-clients alike. The poachers are seeking to improve their own diversity. They often make a work–life balance pitch directed at women who are juggling professional and family responsibilities.

Law firms have implemented a number of best practices for purposes of addressing the work–life balance issue. Many firms have adopted reduced hours policies. These policies will set hours expectations for something like 60 percent of normally expected billable hours, and will compensate based on the same percentage of "normal" compensation. (Note, this equivalence is despite the fact that the firm will likely still incur 100 percent of the fixed costs of such an associate.) A truly enlightened policy will allow for promotion of an associate to partner even while on reduced hours and even if there is no agreed upon date for a return to full time. These policies are called "reduced hours," rather than "part time," because in most practice areas there will be periods during which the demands of the practice will not allow for a fixed schedule, such as Monday through Wednesday. Other policies include generous maternity/paternity leaves (including for adoptions), emergency childcare and re-onboarding programs for lawyers who have been out of the workforce for some period of time for child raising.

Many law firms have robust DEI programs, supported by staff and by committees of partners. Many law firms support organizations such as the Institute for Inclusion in the Legal Profession that encourage the adoption of DEI programs. It is expected that those programs will continue despite threats like one mounted by Senator Tom Cotton. The Arkansas Republican sent letters to fifty-one law firms following Harvard/UNC. Those letters ended with: "To the extent that your firm continues to advise clients regarding DEI programs or operate one of your own, both you and those clients should take care to preserve relevant documents in anticipation of investigations and litigation."[11] It didn't take long for that threatened litigation to come to pass. (Was the senator prescient or simply well informed?) Two law firms were sued in August 2023 by a group backed by the same law firm that brought the Harvard admissions case. The group alleged that the firms' "diversity fellowship" programs are unlawful. Those firms settled the claims against them by modifying the criteria for their fellowships. The pipeline programs described might similarly be in the crosshairs of those opposed to affirmative action and may need to be addressed more specifically to the socioeconomically disadvantaged. In a broader attack on the efforts of the legal profession, in June 2024, twenty-one Republican state attorneys general (AGs) wrote to the ABA asserting that it would need to adjust its criteria for law school accreditation in light of the Harvard/UNC decision, referring to the ABA's standard on diversity and inclusion.

The broadest attacks on the diversity efforts of the legal profession began early in the second Trump administration and were embedded in the March 6, 2025, presidential action entitled "Addressing Risks from Perkins Coie." (Note that Perkins had represented Hillary Clinton in the 2016 campaign.) Section 4(a) of that action directed the chair of the EEOC to "review the [diversity] practices of representative large, influential, or industry leading law firms" and section 4(b) directed the US attorney general to "investigate the practices of large law firms." On March 17, 2025, the acting chair of the EEOC sent a letter to twenty prominent law firms requesting detailed information about their DEI programs.

Other actions that have the effect of reforming meritocracy will aid in retention. If collaboration and collegiality are emphasized and lawyers are encouraged to be humble (that is, to understand that their professional performance and success is enhanced by the support they receive from others within a collaborative and collegial culture), they may be encouraged to reject recruiting efforts by other firms that do not have a similar culture.

One of the critics of meritocracy describes it as a "trap." More specifically, he writes that "Meritocracy entices an anxious and inauthentic elite into a pitiless, lifelong contest to secure income and status through its own excessive industry." He goes on to say that "emancipation from meritocracy . . . would invite the elite . . . to trade diminution in wealth and status that it can easily afford in exchange for a precious increase in leisure and liberty, a reclaiming of an authentic self."[12] This seems a bit dramatic and hyperbolic, especially the "authentic self" part. While many in the elite do identify themselves with their work, how many feel "inauthentic"?

That said, there may be some evidence that, perhaps as a result of introspection born of the pandemic, some individuals working in the private sector are making that trade. Some are engaging in "quiet quitting." And a periodical for the legal profession has declared that the pandemic may have ushered in an "era of disengagement."[13] One author, in describing a "post-career world" had this to say—"Today's workers are increasingly rejecting the script that has long defined the American Dream. They reject the notion that each of us must follow a linear career—lock into a dream early, always climb higher, never stop until you reach the top."[14]

For the many individuals who continue to seek upward mobility and to join the elite, meritocracy encourages striving. While striving is not necessarily such a bad thing for either the individual or his or her firm, it is also clear that in some cases striving can be excessive and lead to "burnout." Burnout is a real issue for professionals of all types and can have a big impact on retention of talent. It is usually caused by something other than simply long hours. Rather, it can be the result of tedium, working with no sense of advancement, or receiving challenging assignments before being ready for them. It can also be the result of work that, while important and financially rewarding, is not emotionally fulfilling at a time when there are so many members of the local community who are visibly in need. It can also be a consequence of "impostor syndrome"—the sense that the individual really doesn't belong in his or her position. (As discussed, this is more likely if the individual believes he or she was hired under a double standard.) For purposes of retention and out of concern for the mental and physical health of colleagues, firms are adopting a variety of practices. These include antidotes to 24/7 connectedness caused by technology, wellness programs, online and on-site counseling, sabbaticals, opportunities for civic engagement (like tutoring or pro bono activities), and—perhaps most important—training of supervisors.

Even senior partners who scoff at trendy psychology theories recognize that there really is such a thing as unconscious bias. They are aware of the experience of symphony orchestras after they adopted "blind" auditions. According to a paper coauthored by the recent economics Nobel laureate, Claudia Goldin, that form of audition resulted in about a quarter of the increase in female orchestra members.[15] So, to enhance the likelihood that compensation and promotion decisions will be made "on the merits," firms provide training to address (or at least acknowledge the possibility of) unconscious bias.

DEFINING AND DETERMINING MERIT

Professional services firms adopt robust definitions of merit with the elements described in chapter 2, for use in assessing professionals for compensation and promotion and to incentivize valued behaviors. Given the nature of the work that law firms engage in for clients and the competitive nature of lawyers, the embedded notions of "collaboration" and "collegiality" are especially important. Professionals who collaborate well with their colleagues lead to better results for clients, because the expertise and experience of different disciplines (and even among those in the same discipline) can be harnessed most effectively. Collegiality is important to collaboration, because it means that different points of view can be shared and debated, as the cliché goes, with "light, not heat." Firm managements can foster collaboration by asking, in the context of annual compensation reviews, questions like, "Which of our colleagues contributed most to your success this past year?" Everyone will want to be named by others in response to that question. Firms with a reputation for collegiality and collaboration often have a competitive advantage in landing assignments involving complex issues, because they will be expected to work well on a cross-disciplinary basis internally and with their counterparts at the client.

As noted, determining whether the elements included in a robust definition of merit have been achieved is a separate issue. Professional services firms typically seek evaluations of their professionals from a broad range of colleagues and discourage evaluations prepared by groups. This approach may mitigate the effects of cognitive bias in making those assessments.

When it comes to deciding which young lawyers merit promotion to partner, law firms can be faced with two distinct issues. The first issue can be characterized as a supply–demand imbalance. A firm may find that it has more young lawyers who arguably meet its standards for promotion than it can promote in a given year without suppressing average partner profitability (which is a public number, thanks to *The American Lawyer* magazine, and can impact a firm's reputation). In that case, the firm may "kick the can down the road" and defer some promotions to a later year. If the problem persists, the firm may seek to outplace individuals to clients and hope that there is no lingering resentment on the part of the un-promoted individual. The second issue is excessive influence over the process by a big producer, who may be motivated by a sense of loyalty to a candidate who has put in thousands of hours (often on nights and weekends) serving the big producer's clients or who has simply become a good friend. If that big producer's favored candidate doesn't meet the firm's standards for promotion, the solution is to appeal to his or her sense of fairness and firm-mindedness.

When it comes to deciding which partners should be placed in management or governance roles, the starting point should be the baseline definition of merit delineated in chapter 2. But that definition may need to be supplemented. If the firm values its culture, the individual should be regarded to be a good exemplar of that culture. If the expectation is that the individual will continue to serve clients, in addition to management duties, the individual should commit to doing so. One of the greatest challenges is resisting placing an individual in such a role if they are big producers, but do not sufficiently meet all elements of the definition of merit.

ADDRESSING MERITOCRATIC INHERITANCE

Firms address meritocratic inheritance in a couple of ways. The most obvious is by adopting a strict anti-nepotism policy—at least when it comes to hiring the children of partners. It's not just the entertainment and celebrity world that can have "nepo babies"! Thought needs to be given to whether the policy affects married couples, given the fact that hardworking young associates might meet their future spouses in the office. Similarly, there is the question of hiring siblings.

Seemingly more difficult is how to address entreaties of clients about hiring a child. Important here is to resist applying a double standard in assessing whether to hire the prospective employee. Among other reasons, this is because terminating such a person who doesn't "work out" can be more damaging to the relationship with a client than not hiring the child in the first place. When the child meets standards and is hired, he or she should be assigned to work only with partners who don't have a relationship with the client. This is in order to reduce the risk that a partner will feel pressure to give glowing evaluations that are not merited.

SUPPRESSING ELITISM

Many law firms, and the individuals who populate them, can rightfully take pride in being among the elite. But as a matter of both internal culture and relationships with their clients, they take steps to suppress elitist tendencies, especially condescension and hubris.

There are a number of best practices relating to internal culture. A firm that reaches out to a broad group of schools in recruiting will explicitly state that once a professional has joined the team, it doesn't matter what school he or she came from. Some firms even have a tradition of discouraging colleagues from putting diplomas on the walls of their offices. Another practice relates to the title of those who are in leadership positions. Many law firms intentionally do not use the title "CEO." Quite common is the title of "chair" of a committee—management, executive, or other. This conveys the notion that there is no single person in charge. It underscores a message of collaboration. And that title is often listed second in the identification of the individual, as in "partner and chair of [name of committee]." This conveys the notion of being a partner (i.e., peer) first.

Then there are the best practices that relate to client relations. Lawyers in these firms are trained to treat their counterparts at the clients with the respect to which they are entitled—that is, as peers to be collaborated with, not folks to be told to stand aside or told what to do. When clients assemble a "virtual firm" to handle a major piece of litigation—with partners from different firms handling different aspects of a case—a failure to collaborate can lead to termination of the assignment. Collaborative relationships will lead to better results for the client. A client who experiences condescension will become a former client. And if things go badly, a high-handed outside lawyer—like an MD with poor bedside manner—is more likely to face a malpractice claim.

PHILANTHROPY

Finally, professional services firms and individual partners in those firms engage in philanthropy. This can be because of client demands. Or it can be to aid in recruiting, as is the case of law firms establishing scholarships and professorial chairs at law schools. Or it can assist in retention by giving professionals an outlet for their own civic engagement, as is the case with involvement in "adopt-a-school" programs. Finally, it can be viewed simply as a professional responsibility, as is the case with pro bono services. Many of these efforts, together with pipeline programs, can advance equal opportunity.

RESULTS

While the professional services firms have established a number of best practices, it is appropriate to take a clear-eyed look at how successful those practices have been in addressing one of the areas of greatest need in reforming meritocracy—namely, inclusion. While the precise numbers vary by profession, the simplified answer is this: For all but investment banking and medicine, the percentage of women in the profession roughly parallels the percentage of women in the population. In only accounting and consulting are minorities represented in a percentage consistent with their percentage in the population. Among minorities, Black professionals are significantly underrepresented in all but consulting.

The "bad old days" described at the beginning of this chapter are behind the law firms, and thoughtful programs have been developed and energetically pursued to advance diversity and inclusion. Moreover, most firms have taken a zero-tolerance approach when reacting to credible claims of sexual harassment—by colleagues or, even, clients. Nevertheless, there continue to be challenges in achieving meaningful results even at the most well-meaning of firms. For example, while the percentage of women in law firms roughly parallels the percentage of women in the population, a sophisticated look requires understanding the percentage of women who are partners or in leadership positions. Representation of women and minorities has improved, but is still lagging. The National Association for Law Placement (NALP) publishes reports on women and minorities in US law firms of all sizes. Those reports indicate that minorities represented 2.95 percent of partners in 1997, 8.42 percent in 2017, and 11.4 percent in 2022. Women represented 14.21 percent of partners in 1997, 22.70 percent in 2017, and 26.7 percent in 2022. Nevertheless, in its March 2024 bulletin, NALP observed that "women and partners of color remain substantially underrepresented within the partnership ranks."[16]

While law firms will note that their most successful women and minority partners are often recruited away by clients, that is clearly not a complete explanation.

In some instances, the failure to achieve more in the way of diversity and inclusion may be a function of an absence of total buy-in by all of the partners of professional services firms. Some may be unconvinced of the sincerity, or efficacy, of avoiding a double standard in hiring and promotion and, as a result, believe that efforts at diversity and inclusion sow the seeds for later claims of discrimination. Aside from diligence in avoiding a double standard, the best arguments to use in trying to persuade diversity skeptics appeal to self-interest. First, professional services firms are in the business of helping clients solve problems. Having access to a diversity of points of view and experience will make the professionals better problem-solvers. If that is too ethereal an argument, the second argument usually carries the day—clients are demanding diversity on the teams that advise them. And clients have gotten more sophisticated over time in policing the diversity of their teams. It is not enough just to show up to meetings with a diverse team in tow. Because many professional services firms bill on the basis of time, clients ask for an analysis of the time spent by women and minority lawyers on their matters. Client demands regarding diversity are now being downplayed in light of recent attacks on DEI.

A BRIEF DIGRESSION ABOUT ANOTHER ORGANIZATION OF PROFESSIONALS

One might not expect to pick up lessons about reforming meritocracy from the National Football League, but consider the following. In terms of being open to, and benefiting from, an expansion of the pool of talent, consider how far the teams in the NFL have come from the days when all quarterbacks were white. In fact, those days were not so long ago. Although there were Black quarterbacks as early as 1979, the movie *Any Given Sunday* suggested that they were something of a unicorn as late as 1999. That movie's plot twist involved the unexpected success of a Black third-string NFL quarterback who was given his chance when the white starter and the white backup were injured. (Twenty-five years later, half of the starting QBs in the league are Black.) In terms of thoughtfully pursuing affirmative action while resisting application of a double standard, look at the adoption and application of the Rooney Rule for filling head coaching positions. The application of the Rooney Rule was subsequently broadened to other positions. In addition to being very vocal about its commitment to diversity, the NFL created concrete rewards for teams—"compensatory draft picks"—when they "lose a minority coach or executive to a head coach or general manager job with another team."[17] In terms of encouraging philanthropy, consider the Walter Payton Man of the Year Award. In terms of resisting credentialism, consider the success of Bill Belichick in going with Tom Brady—the 199th pick from the sixth round of the 2000 NFL draft.[18] And then there are numerous examples of ignoring those who criticize "wokeness"—the end zones and backs of helmets that display the words "end racism"; and the statement issued after the murder of George Floyd that "we were wrong for not listening to NFL players earlier. . . . We, the NFL, believe Black Lives Matter."[19] While the post-Floyd statement did not mention Colin Kaepernick by name, the reference to encouraging peaceful protest was as validating as Nike's ads. Then came the year-round social justice initiative called "Inspire Change." Perhaps the example of the NFL will inspire change in corporate America!

7

MERITOCRACY IN CORPORATE AMERICA

Before getting into how corporate America can adopt and expand upon the best practices of the professional services firms, a threshold question needs to be addressed: Is it appropriate for leaders of corporate America (and especially public companies) to take on reforming meritocracy . . . at least within their own organizations? This question has three components. The first has already been asked and answered—should reform come from the private sector rather than the government? For reasons already articulated, my answer is a resounding "yes!" The other two components are these—can leaders of corporate America take this on in keeping with fiduciary duties to shareholders; will managements be accused of being "woke" by doing so (and does that matter)?

FIDUCIARY DUTIES

Corporate boards and managements are required to make decisions for the benefit of the shareholders. This obligation is embodied in the notion of a generalized fiduciary duty to the corporation and shareholders. This is not to say that there are no duties to the non-shareholder stakeholders (sometimes called the "other constituencies")—employees, creditors, customers, suppliers, and communities. Those duties are set forth in specific statutes, regulations, and contracts and are also derived from tort law. Actions that are not required by those specific obligations and that benefit the other constituencies are allowed so long as the decision-makers have reached a rational business judgment, in compliance with their duties of care and loyalty, that those actions have a nexus with long-term shareholder value. The legitimacy of this approach is reflected in the methodology applied by the Drucker Institute in its annual "Management Top 250" rankings, which are published by *The Wall Street Journal*. That ranking system covers "five dimensions of corporate performance," with the greatest weight (24 percent) in 2024 given to "social responsibility"—ahead of customer satisfaction (22 percent), innovation (21 percent), employee engagement (20 percent), and financial strength (13 percent).[1] If the shareholders do not agree with the decision, their remedy is to replace the corporate board. Bottom line: Corporate boards and managements can, absolutely, take thoughtfully considered steps that have the effect of reforming meritocracy.[2]

That is the law of fiduciary duties in a nutshell. It should be noted that the shareholder versus stakeholder debate has gone on, literally, for over a century. While not consistent with current law, some commentators have even advocated that actions for the benefit of stakeholders do not need to be justified by a nexus with shareholder value. This position is based on the notion that, because the corporate form (and its benefits in terms of limited liability and facilitation of the ability to raise capital) is based on a grant from the state, a corporation has an obligation to society and not just its owners.[3]

Set forth in appendix C is a chronology of the shareholder versus stakeholder debate. It begins with the 1919 decision in *Dodge v. Ford*. Perhaps the best-known event captured on the chronology is the 1970 article in *The New York Times Magazine* by Milton Friedman entitled "The Social Responsibility of Business Is to Increase Profits."[4] Entries from 1981, 1997, and 2019 show how the Business Roundtable positions have ebbed and flowed.

"WOKE" ATTACKS

The adoption by corporate America of some of the best practices of professional services firms—especially those designed to increase the pool of talent by making it more inclusive and diverse—might generate an attack for "wokeness." One extreme version was the suggestion that the failure of Silicon Valley Bank somehow involved the diversity of its board of directors and its DEI stance.[5] And Elon Musk, after the door panel flew off an in-flight Alaska Airlines 737, "claimed in a series of posts on X that [efforts by United Airlines and Boeing to hire non-white pilots and factory workers] have made air travel less safe," but "offered no evidence for the claim."[6] (Echoing Musk, in response to the tragic midair collision at Reagan National Airport at the end of January 2025 and before there had been any investigation as to the cause of the accident, President Trump blamed DEI programs, particularly at the Federal Aviation Administration. Like Musk, he cited no evidence. When asked for the basis of his conclusion, he said "Because I have common sense.")[7] Another example was an opinion piece in *The Wall Street Journal*, reacting to Goldman Sachs' encouraging leaders to "embrace a full rainbow range of 'pronouns.'" That piece went on to describe "the rising numbers of identity-box-checking drones who help enforce the unspoken rules of woke compliance."[8] Even Chick-fil-A, which in the past was criticized by progressives for its conservative social positions, has been accused of "going woke" because of a corporate policy supportive of "a culture of belonging" appearing on its website.[9] Finally, there have been recent examples of activist shareholders putting forth proposals, using Rule 14a-8 of the Securities and Exchange Commission in opposition to DEI programs, as well as threats of litigation against companies unless they retract DEI policies and activities.

Leaders of corporate America need to be thoughtful and deliberate in considering how to respond to a "woke" attack. They should consider the risk that succumbing to pressure from "anti-woke" activists can result in blowback from investors that support corporate commitments to DEI and environmental, social, and governance (ESG) positions.[10] It may also be the case that the anti-woke activists do not speak for the majority of Americans—who are, after all, the customer or ultimate consumers of the products and services of corporate America. Consider the results of a survey done by the Harris Poll on behalf of the Black Economic Alliance Foundation. Nearly 80 percent of those surveyed "support businesses taking active steps to make sure companies reflect the diversity of the American population," including "67 percent of Republicans, 76 percent of Independents, and 90 percent of Democrats."[11]

Moreover, corporate fiduciaries should not turn over decision-making to (or be inappropriately influenced by) activist shareholders who have no fiduciary duty to the corporation or its shareholders. Similarly, they shouldn't turn over decision-making to (or be inappropriately influenced by) demagogic politicians, cable news bloviators, social media posters, or others. So, if the adoption or continuation of DEI programs could advance the long-term best interests of the shareholders, there should be no hesitation in giving them serious consideration through a carefully executed corporate governance process (to be described). Even though the Supreme Court did not defer to the universities' judgments about the optimal student body, there should be a deferral to the business judgment of corporate leadership about what is in their shareholders' best interests.

Despite enhanced scrutiny of corporate DEI policies (and even litigation) following the Harvard/UNC decision, it has been reported that "many companies [especially those marketing consumer goods] are reinforcing their commitment to diversity, equity, and inclusion practices, calling them critical to their businesses."[12] Costco provides a great example of this commitment. It received a shareholder proposal seeking a vote at its 2025 annual meeting to require a "report on the risks of maintaining DEI efforts." In the section of its proxy statement, Costco's board of directors unanimously recommended against the proposal, stating that they "believe our commitment to an enterprise rooted in respect and inclusion is appropriate and necessary," that "our success . . . has been built on service to our critical stakeholders," and that "our efforts around diversity, equity, and inclusion follow our code of ethics." The board further asserted that "the proponent's broader agenda is not reducing risk for the company but abolition of diversity initiatives."[13] Costco's bold stance may represent an exception. A few days before the presidential inauguration of 2025, a front-page article in *The Wall Street Journal* (with the subheading "Diversity, Climate Initiatives Gutted") reported: "From Meta to McDonald's to Wall Street, America's corporate bosses aren't waiting for the January 20 inauguration to start conforming with views favored in the Trump 2.0 universe."[14] And on January 21, 2025, in his second day back in office, President Trump (as part of his flurry of executive orders) signed an executive order that, among other things, requires all executive departments and agencies of the federal government "to combat illegal private-sector DEI preferences, mandates, policies, programs, and activities."[15] Perhaps in an effort to have it both ways while under pressure from a conservative activist, John Deere announced on X, formerly known as Twitter, that it would "no longer participate in or support external social or cultural awareness parades, festivals, or events" and it would be "auditing all company-mandated training materials and policies to ensure the absence of socially motivated messages," yet in the same message it stated that "we fundamentally believe that a diverse workforce enables us to best meet our customers' needs."[16]

Efforts in the name of ESG are also under attack for "wokeness." Those attacks from some investors, conservative groups, and politicians are reported to be causing companies to reduce mentioning those efforts on earnings calls and to consider pulling back from the initiatives. This is despite the fact that "70 percent of the global chief executives said that their company's ESG programs improve their financial performance," according to a 2022 KPMG survey.[17]

• • •

So, let's look at the best practices of professional services firms (many of which have already been adopted by companies) and consider how they might be adopted and amplified by all companies in corporate America.

INCREASING THE POOL OF TALENT BY MAKING IT MORE INCLUSIVE

As to recruiting, some companies are already taking steps to address one version of credentialism by eliminating the requirement for a four-year degree in screening applicants for positions that really don't require such a degree. This approach is espoused by a group called Tear the Paper Ceiling. (That group, like the college admissions group mentioned in chapter 3, uses the acronym STARs—standing in this instance for "skilled through alternative routes.") The Business Roundtable endorsed this approach with its "Multiple Pathways Initiative" announced in 2022.[18] This approach is sometimes labeled "skills-based hiring." A study published by the Burning Glass Institute reported that "for all its fanfare, the increased opportunity promised by Skills-Based Hiring was borne out not even in one of seven hundred hires last year 2022" and "the net effect is a change of only 0.14 percentage points in incremental hiring of candidates without degrees."[19] So, more needs to be done to advance a good theory into effective practice.

Companies that recruit on campuses should consider sending recruiters to a broad group of schools, including historically Black colleges and universities (HBCUs). Companies should consider partnering with universities that offer "co-op programs," such as Northeastern, Drexel, and Georgia Tech.[20] Because placements under those programs are compensated, co-ops, like paid internships, are more likely to expand the pool of available talent by providing opportunities to students for whom the cost of higher education is a challenge.

Folks in the C-suite should learn how to resist efforts from their customers and networks seeking to bestow meritocratic inheritance, especially if that would involve applying a double standard in favor of underqualified children of affluence. Such efforts may be at an all-time high because "employers are drowning in job applications" and "to stand out, job seekers need to know someone who can pluck their résumé out of the digital slush pile."[21] It is worth noting that failing to resist such efforts can, under some circumstances, involve a conflict of interest or a violation of a code of conduct. If regulators or governmental officials are involved, anticorruption statutes (including the Foreign Corrupt Practices Act [FCPA]) could be implicated. For example, in 2016, JPMorgan settled SEC charges "that it . . . corruptly influenced government officials in the Asia-Pacific region by giving jobs and internships to their relatives and friends" and "engaged in a systematic bribery scheme by hiring children of government officials . . . who were typically unqualified for the positions on their own merit," all in violation of the FCPA.[22]

Companies should adopt pipeline programs. Many already have: United Flight School; DuPont for chemical engineers; Edison International's scholars program for STEM studies. Other companies have enhanced recruiting by creating white-collar training programs that operate like an apprenticeship—McDonald's; Accenture; JPMorgan Chase; Aon; Walmart. Then there is the Google Professional Certificates program, run by Coursera, that promises to teach skills for careers in "Data Analytics, Digital Marketing & E-commerce, IT Support, Project Management, or UX Design."[23] And the Home Depot program called "Path to Pro" provides free training for those who wish to enter the construction trades.[24]

A caveat: To the extent that alternatives to a four-year diploma make the American Dream accessible to a larger group of individuals, they are clearly worthwhile. However, it remains the case that four years of college have enormous benefits. At the right institutions, students receive an education that goes beyond simply a transfer of information and the development of marketable skills. Those students learn to think and problem-solve. They learn how to learn, which facilitates a lifetime of intellectual growth. For many, it provides an opportunity to mature and live relatively independently. There continues to be a lifelong financial benefit to the degree. And a four-year degree remains a requirement for certain professions and is a near necessity for joining the elite in a well-operating meritocracy—although that degree need not be from an Ivy-plus college or other highly selective institution. Further, it has been argued that "there are a host of benefits . . . from higher education that enrich society as a whole . . . [including] its ability to cultivate the sort of informed and active citizenship that lies at the heart of a vibrant democracy."[25] In short, it would be a shame for high-potential young men and women (especially from minority groups) to "settle" for anything less, and they should not be encouraged to do so.

As to talent development and retention: Robust training programs are obviously an element of talent development. Such programs are also attractive for recruiting and retention. An investment in talent development implies the presence of a "corporate ladder," which is also attractive. One company has made a commitment to a corporate ladder more explicit. Nath Inc., a hotel operator, created "a career-development program with cross-department training and leadership workshops. Prospective housekeepers liked the idea that the company offered a path from cleaning rooms to . . . managing a hotel."[26] A tradition of internal promotions (rather than always seeking external candidates) can also benefit a company by avoiding the potential downside of "chasing stars" from the outside. ("Chasing stars" is the term used by Boris Groysberg in his book of the same name, with the subtitle "The Myth of Talent and the Portability of Performance." He cautions that success of an individual in one organization does not necessarily mean they will succeed in a new organization, because there can be cultural differences and a different support environment.)[27] When technology and automation make some employees redundant, some companies are providing retraining. Mentoring programs work in all contexts and can be especially important to employees whose backgrounds make them unfamiliar with a corporate setting. Issues of burnout and unconscious bias are not limited, by any means, to professional service firms.

A "Blue Ribbon Commission" of the National Association of Corporate Directors has urged public company boards to oversee talent development and retention, as part of its "responsibility to help ensure that the company is appropriately developing talent to meet expected future needs."[28] In response, the charters of many board compensation committees have been expanded. The broadening of the charters is reflected in the new titles of the committees—for example: "Leadership Development and Compensation Committee" (Amazon); "Compensation and Talent Committee" (McKesson); "People and Compensation Committee" (PG&E); "People, Culture and Compensation Committee" (Manpower). Many boards are adopting a practice of giving members of middle management more exposure to directors than occasional appearances at board meetings—either at the traditional pre-meeting dinner of the entire board or through lunches arranged for one or a few directors to meet with a similar number of those middle managers.

Corporate boards should also be aware of another finding of the study released by the Center for Talent Innovation in 2019: More than one in three Black employees intended to leave their companies, and Black employees are 30 percent more likely to intend to leave than their white counterparts.[29] Having greater racial diversity in the boardroom may be a way to counter this trend. (This was mandated by a California statute, held to be unconstitutional in May 2023, and encouraged by a Nasdaq disclosure requirement, struck down at the end of 2024 by a federal court, having also been challenged by twenty-two state attorneys general.)[30] Black directors can serve as role models, and they are frequently more attuned to the progress of Black professionals within the company. Moreover, their presence is a reflection of the commitment of the company to diversity—not just of race, but also diversity of thought and experience that can be a valuable commodity in decision-making.[31]

Another of the findings of that survey, already mentioned, was that both white and Black employees found DEI programs of their employers to be generally ineffective. This is another subject for the attention of the board and its HR committee.

DEFINING AND DETERMINING MERIT

Recruiters should apply a definition of merit that appropriately captures the attributes that will make a candidate a good future employee. For most organizations, the elements of merit described in chapter 2 will be at least a good starting point. Those elements may need to be tweaked, or even supplemented, depending on the organization's specific context and challenges.

A broad definition of merit should be applied in compensation and promotion decisions. Evaluations for these purposes should touch on all relevant elements. Evaluations may benefit from following the approach of 360-degree feedback—soliciting views of peers and subordinates, not just superiors. This feedback is especially useful for assessing collaboration and collegiality and can negate the risk of inappropriately rewarding a "kiss up, kick down" employee. (Possible additions to the definition to be considered in the context of CEO succession decisions will be discussed later.)

SUPPRESSING ELITISM

Condescension and hubris on the part of the elite has been identified as one of the flaws of the current version of meritocracy. As noted earlier, for a professional services firm, elitism needs to be addressed as a matter of internal culture and external relationships. It is no less important an issue for companies in corporate America, although the different context suggests somewhat different approaches. Most professional services firms have a relatively flat hierarchy and organization chart (at least formally). For example, law firms have partners and associates (and sometimes a category called "counsel"). In contrast, the management structures of companies in corporate America tend to be much more pyramidal—there is the C-suite (those executives whose titles begin with the word "chief"); an array of vice presidents, assistant VPs; and so on.

The demeanor of individuals throughout an organization toward their colleagues and support staff is often a reflection of the demeanor of a small number of people at the top of the organization, namely the members of the C-suite—especially the CEO. If that demeanor is one of condescension and hubris, it can adversely impact collaboration and collegiality and, as a result, personnel retention—shrinking the pool of available talent. That kind of demeanor can also have a negative impact on risk management, by discouraging individuals from passing along to superiors bad news (or new information or analysis) early enough so that something can be done to address nascent problems.

The wrong kind of demeanor can also affect the company's overall reputation and relations with the outside world. A high-handed attitude by its representatives toward its community, suppliers, and regulators can redound to the company's detriment. If nothing else, at a time of crisis (inevitable for just about any company), that kind of attitude may discourage giving the company a break.

A company that is viewed as elitist because it is closely associated with the velvet rope economy might consider broadening the cohort of beneficiaries to include groups like first responders, teachers, active military, and veterans. Airlines already provide early boarding for the active military.

CORPORATE PHILANTHROPY

Just like professional services firms, corporations can engage in philanthropy. In many instances, this leads to reputation enhancement. The Sara Lee art donation was already mentioned. Another example is the 1987 decision by Merck, the huge US pharmaceutical company, to donate an unlimited amount of Mectizan to eliminate river blindness in Africa and Latin America. Some philanthropy (including matching donations made by employees and giving employees paid time off to participate in community-building endeavors) aids in recruiting and retention. When philanthropy follows a corporate crisis and is targeted to communities affected by the crisis, it may be perceived as a form of reputation washing. So long as philanthropy serves a corporate purpose, it cannot be successfully attacked as waste. Problems can arise, however, when philanthropy is perceived to be motivated largely to benefit individuals within the corporation.

CORPORATE GOVERNANCE PROCESS

Over the past few years, managements that were considering speaking out or taking a position on an issue of the day or an issue otherwise embroiled in the culture wars learned that they needed to involve their boards of directors in a thoughtful consideration of a variety of questions—Is silence an option? What will be the blowback and do the benefits outweigh the costs? Indeed, can we fully anticipate the extent of blowback in an age of extreme social divisiveness when social media can so effectively organize a consumer boycott (think Bud Light)? Is blowback a more serious risk for companies that sell consumer goods than for companies that sell to other companies? What can we do to minimize the blowback? Can a position taken by a CEO be effectively characterized as personal, not corporate? And so on.[32]

Similarly, when management is considering taking actions to reform meritocracy in their own organization, it should involve the board. This is for several reasons. First, taking such actions can have an operational impact. Second, in many ways meritocracy is all about talent management, which (as discussed) a board is increasingly expected to oversee. Third, such actions can have a reputational impact—positive or negative—because by design or otherwise they are unlikely to be matters communicated only internally.

The questions that should be considered by management and the board end with an overarching one: Do we anticipate that the actions will make us a stronger company and will provide long-term benefits to the shareholders? This will be answered based on consideration of a more detailed set of questions. What will be the short-term costs if we decide on one or more of the following: enhancing training, establishing a pipeline program, providing more corporate philanthropy, reestablishing a corporate ladder with the effect of losing the cost savings of outsourcing, and similar measures and other actions? Are we committed to enhancing diversity without application of a double standard, and do we have a credible plan for doing so? What will be the reactions of current and prospective future employees? Will our actions be consistent with those of our peers, or will we be standing out, either in a good way or not? Do we have a plan for what and how we intend to communicate what we are doing, both internally and externally?

CEO SUCCESSION

Selecting a CEO is the ultimate test of meritocracy in corporate America.

As noted in chapter 2, the baseline definition of merit needs to be supplemented when determining who should be the CEO of an organization. There are three additional elements that should be considered in deciding on CEO succession.

First, a CEO candidate should be committed to meritocracy. Having a CEO who is not committed to meritocracy might result in a "weak bench" and hamper the performance of the organization.

That emphasis could be motivated by not wanting to feel threatened by the presence of a readily available successor. Or, the CEO could be displaying excessive loyalty, and granting tenure, to original members of the team whose skills and energy level have not kept up with the growth and complexity of the organization. CEOs who are committed to meritocracy, and confident of their positions, will also serve as mentors to those in their organizations who are potential successors or who could go on to be CEOs elsewhere.

Second, leadership skill is critical and is an attribute that includes, but goes well beyond, management skill. In his classic *On Leadership*, John Gardner delineates nine tasks that he describes as the "most significant functions of leadership"—envisioning goals; affirming values; motivating others; managing (including agenda setting); achieving unity on the team; explaining; serving as a symbol; representing the group; and renewing their organizations to adjust to internal and external changes. Leadership also involves the ability to gain "followership."[33] An individual who is selflessly ambitious, humble, and respectful will be more likely to attract followers.

Finally, the ability to lead and operate effectively during a crisis is important. This is because there is a reasonable probability that the company will go through one crisis or another during the CEO's tenure. There are two elements of this—an ability to handle stress (including the strength of character to resist taking shortcuts); and an ability to adjust leadership style during the pendency of the crisis. For example, exhaustive analysis and a goal of near unanimity may need to be supplanted by decisiveness in a time of crisis.[34]

In assessing a candidate, the board should also be careful not to overemphasize certain criteria, such as formal credentials, charisma, or even communications skills. These are important, of course, but can be overemphasized. And, crediting non-merit factors—such as a candidate's personal relationship with one or more members of the board and even physical appearance[35]—should be resisted.

Some of the elements of merit may be difficult for a board to assess. Moreover, assessing an external candidate can be more difficult than assessing an internal candidate. Among other things, due diligence is often limited, regarding external candidates, because they are typically employed elsewhere and do not want their employer to know that they are considering a move. That makes it difficult to determine whether an external candidate has been successful largely because of the support of others and the particular culture of his or her current employer. It makes it more difficult to understand the candidate's reputation with his or her peers and whether the candidate is the type who will gain followership.

For either an internal or an external candidate, some boards have asked a psychologist or psychiatrist to interview the leading candidate. This is sometimes called a "cultural assessment," but character is also being assessed. Such a professional can provide surprisingly good insights.

There is a caveat to all of this—people change over time. Some, for the better. Many CEOs become more self-assured and better listeners. Regrettably, others deserve the quip made by Jack Fuller, a good friend (and Pulitzer Prize winning journalist before he went to the "corporate side")—"CEO can be a progressive disease."

If a board has done a thorough job in selecting the new CEO and is convinced of the wisdom of its decision, it should consider taking steps designed to assist in the transition to new leadership. This is because even a candidate carefully selected on the merits can fail if subverted.

First and foremost is the question of the role of the outgoing CEO. Should he or she remain on the board, either as a board chair or as a director, and if so for how long? Should he or she keep an office at the corporate headquarters, and if so, how long? Does he or she harbor the hope of becoming a "boomerang" CEO? Can he or she deal with going from "who's who to who are you"?

Second, some selections of a new CEO create disappointed "also-rans," resulting in at least two potential problems. Will the also-rans leave the company, to its detriment, or will they remain and possibly undermine the successor? As to the former, a savvy new CEO will try the Abe Lincoln "team of rivals" approach. As to the latter, the most extreme solution was effected in the GE succession of 2001. The three candidates were told by Jack Welch that one of them would become CEO and the other two fired.

FAMILY-CONTROLLED COMPANIES

CEO succession in family-controlled companies can resemble Jefferson's "artificial aristocracy founded on wealth and birth." That can be as much of a "mischievous ingredient" in business as it is in government. This, of course, is not always the case. There have been many examples of sons and daughters who were spectacularly successful successors. Moreover, there is an element of legitimacy to selecting family members of the majority owners, in the sense of solving the "agency problem" through the convergence of "ownership and control."[36] That legitimacy is diminished, of course, when voting control is not accompanied by an equal economic interest. This is the case when there is a dual-class capital structure that gives a higher vote to one class of shares and, for example, gives 80 percent of the vote to a family that has only 20 percent of an economic stake.

Whether majority voting power is based on majority economic ownership or otherwise, dealing with a family's desire to promote one of its members to CEO can present a real challenge to independent directors on a board of directors. Even if a majority are independent, those directors understand that going against the wishes of the family can result in losing their seat. Nevertheless, they also realize that they have a fiduciary duty to the corporation and all of its shareholders. If the family's candidate does meet the broadened definition of merit described, the integrity and commitment to meritocracy of the independent directors, as well as their powers of persuasion, will be put to the test. In some cases, if directors are unable to succeed in making their case against promoting a family member, they will simply resign.

When the board of a family-controlled company is confident in its selection, it needs to pay particular attention to the possibility of intra-family rivalries—especially in the second or third generation after the founder. Again, even a perfect candidate's success can be subverted.

CEO succession is not the only area of meritocratic challenge in a family-controlled company. Similar issues can arise when the family wishes to place a younger member in a position of responsibility (for example, as CFO) before he or she is ready or, worse, when there are serious questions about whether they would ever be ready. And even if the family member is ready and able to serve in a particular position, non-family employees can have concerns about whether their career opportunities will be unfairly stifled. There can also be issues of putting such a person on the board of directors.

All of these complications, and the alternative path of a sale, lead to the perhaps unsurprising statistics that "only 30 percent of family businesses make it to the second generation, 12 percent into the third generation, and 3 percent into the fourth generation."[37]

8

THE BROADER ROLE OF LEADERS FROM THE PRIVATE SECTOR

If leaders of professional services firms and corporate America wish to help reform meritocracy more broadly (that is, outside the four walls of their organizations), they often will have the opportunity to do so. They can have a great deal of influence over institutions of higher learning, as trustees and as donors. Their influence in the political sphere can be asserted through campaign donations and public endorsements. Finally, as prominent citizens of their own communities and through service on school boards and the boards of civic and charitable institutions, they can help initiate and fund programs that advance, and help eliminate barriers to, equal opportunity. Set forth in this chapter are some possible items for their attention. Even if these actions may yield improvements only at the margins, they are worth taking. In addition, sincere efforts—and not simply lip service—just might help redeem the reputation of the elite.

Repeating an earlier caveat: For some of these initiatives—and even those pursued on a "personal," not institutional, level—it would be prudent for the leaders to observe good corporate governance practices and consult with their boards, especially before spending corporate resources or associating the corporate name with their activities.

For this reason, and because they will likely have more available time, it may be that retired private-sector leaders will be in the best position to encourage reform. For example, the average age of S&P 500 CEOs at the time they step down from that role is early to mid-sixties.[1] While many who actually retire at that age are occupied with public company board seats, the limitations on "overboarding" may make time available for them to be active with institutions of higher learning and in their communities, even if they have no inclinations to be active in the political sphere.

The potential for this kind of involvement on the part of retiring leaders has led to programs such as the "Leadership and Society Initiative" put on by the Graham School at the University of Chicago. The yearlong program "supports accomplished executives in successfully transitioning from their long-standing careers toward purposeful next chapters of leadership for society." The inaugural class included twenty-five individuals, mostly former members of C-suites.[2]

The key words, however, are "involvement" and "active." Current and former leaders will have the greatest impact if they do more—much more—than just lend their names to a board. Financial contributions are, of course, always welcome. But sharing their experience, expertise, and sage advice—all forms of "sweat equity"—can be even more valuable. And helping the organization stay focused on its core mission, in addition to its financial stability, is critical.[3]

UNIVERSITIES

As noted in the introduction to this volume, the first step for the achievement of a meritocratic society is to provide access to quality education for a broad segment of the population. A leader interested in advancing this goal in a university might support a variety of policies.

Test-optional admissions is the lowest hanging fruit, as more than 80 percent of schools adopted this policy.[4] (The pros and cons—and adoption and abandonment—of this policy have been discussed earlier.) Less common, and more difficult from a financial standpoint, is a policy of need-blind admissions. This, of course, is easier said than done. Simply knowing the zip code of an applicant, or the occupation of his or her parent(s), provides fairly accurate insight into need or no-need. And in recessionary periods, this policy can present a real financial challenge.[5]

Eliminating legacy admissions preferences (as Hopkins, Wesleyan, Amherst, MIT, and others have done) is a recent hot topic for opinion pieces and general debate, with commentators coming down forcefully on both sides of the issue. Doing so will directly address meritocratic inheritance, but it can also have an adverse effect on alumni relations and fundraising. That said, there may be no choice. The ink was barely dry on the Harvard/UNC decision before a lawsuit was filed seeking to ban legacy admission preferences as a form of unlawful affirmative action benefiting white applicants. Nearly as quickly, the US Department of Education announced an investigation, prompted by a civil rights complaint from Latino and Black advocacy groups, into Harvard's legacy (and donor) admissions preferences.[6] It is also worth noting that in 2023, a bill was introduced in the Massachusetts legislature proposing an up to 0.2 percent tax on endowments at universities that consider legacy status in their admissions processes.[7] Finally, in 2024, California banned colleges in that state from "providing a legacy preference or donor preference, to an applicant" for admission. It joined several other states in doing so, and there may be a bipartisan push in Congress for a federal ban.[8]

There are a number of issues relating to admissions that deserve careful study:

- Do early action and early decision admissions programs benefit affluent students because the admissions decision and a requirement to commit precede the financial aid decision? Do these programs essentially negate attempts at "need-blind" admissions (which may be an illusory promise in any event)? Should a college consider adopting a "need affirmative" admissions policy, as proposed by Professor Chetty and his colleagues? Can a school maintain a financial aid program available only to certain minorities? Note that in August 2023, a complaint was filed against Kansas State University with the Office for Civil Rights of the US Department of Education, attacking its $700 scholarships for students of "historically underrepresented backgrounds," with "special preference" for "applicants of African American, American Indian, Asian American, and Latinx American heritage."[9]

- Do admissions preferences for athletes in certain sports—golf, fencing, tennis, sailing, etc.—benefit affluent students because participation in those sports is largely unavailable to students from a socioeconomically disadvantaged family? But would elimination of those sports or preferences potentially create challenges under Title IX?
- Should the university adopt a policy to prohibit the development office from having any discussions with a family that has a student with a pending application?
- It is anticipated that colleges will develop work-arounds to explicit racially based affirmative action in the aftermath of the decision in the Harvard/UNC cases, in order to maintain diversity in their entering classes. In that regard, trustees should be aware of the "Dear Colleague" letter (and related Q and A) issued in August 2023 by the US Departments of Justice and Education in which the Biden administration announced that it "stands ready to support institutions that recognize that . . . [racial and ethnic] diversity is core to their commitment to excellence." The departments encouraged "redoubling efforts to recruit and retain talented students from underserved communities" and a "greater focus on fostering a sense of belonging for [such] students currently enrolled."[10] That said, will such efforts withstand inevitable constitutional challenge?
- Does a diverse student body enhance or detract from free expression and free speech on campus, as championed by the Chicago

Principles? One extreme view from the Right: "The controversies over freedom of expression in the academy will not end until university presidents, trustees, and faculties abandon sustained diversity as one of their core missions."[11] A bit more temperate view was reflected in a Gallup poll that found that 76 percent of college students think these concepts are frequently or occasionally in conflict.[12] Christopher Eisgruber, the president of Princeton University, had this to say on the subject in 2020: "We are in an era when many people mistakenly treat free speech and inclusivity as competing values."[13] Or as John Palfrey, the former head of school at Phillips Andover and current CEO of the MacArthur Foundation, has observed—"The American experiment is, at its highest form, about diversity and free expression coexisting. That coexistence has not been easy, nor has it been all that successful . . ." and "the idea of diversity and free expression opposing one another may serve some immediate political purpose, but it will not serve our society in the long run."[14] One way to encourage free expression is for teachers to ask their students to adhere to the Chatham House Rule when reporting to others (on social media or otherwise) about discussions in the classroom. That rule allows reporting about what was said, but not who said what. While expecting perfect adherence to the rule may be Pollyannaish, and enforcement mechanisms may be largely unavailable, there is a hope that students will feel a moral obligation or at least peer pressure to follow the rule.

A diverse student body is not the only goal. Racial and gender diversity of the faculty is an important goal. One of the risks associated with allegedly utilizing a double standard to achieve that goal is illustrated by a recent lawsuit filed against Northwestern Pritzker School of Law. That suit, brought by a conservative group calling itself "Faculty, Alumni, and Students Opposed to Racial Preferences" alleges that the leadership of the law school "has propagated and enforced a mandate to hire as many non-white and non-male faculty candidates as possible" and "intentionally and consciously discriminated . . . against white men who are heterosexual." In support of this allegation, the plaintiff cited purported instances where less qualified minority candidates were hired over highly qualified white men. The first sentence of the complaint speaks more broadly, and breathlessly: "Faculty hiring at American universities is a cesspool of corruption and lawlessness."[15]

An ideologically diverse faculty is also important. University trustees should ask this: Is there a reasonable balance among our faculty between liberals and conservatives? In his commencement address to the 2014 graduates at Harvard, Mike Bloomberg noted that "in the 2012 presidential race . . . 96 percent of all campaign contributions from Ivy League faculty and employees went to Barack Obama." He went on to caution that "a university cannot be great if its faculty is politically homogeneous" and that "great universities must not become predictably partisan."[16] If "ideological diversity" is too political-sounding, try the more "innocuous, bureaucratic-sounding" version—viewpoint diversity.[17]

Leaders who are trustees or donors will often be asked by acquaintances in their business or social networks to assist in gaining admission for the children of those acquaintances. Whether or not those children meet the institution's standards for admission, providing such assistance is an example of meritocratic inheritance. When a child does not meet those standards, exerting influence to help him or her gain admission is clearly inconsistent with meritocracy, is probably not in the best interest of the child, and may violate a trustee's duty to the institution. Many trustees will have a personal policy not to write a letter of recommendation without having some firsthand knowledge of the applicant—best, familiarity gained over a long time period, but at a minimum through a personal interview. When that knowledge suggests to the trustee that the candidate does not meet standards, the trustee should have sufficient personal integrity to decline to write a letter. When standards are met, the letter should be low key—simply a data point for the admissions office—not a request for favorable action.

Trustees who want their universities to be engines of upward mobility should focus their financial support on scholarship programs for the economically disadvantaged. (Less ego boosting perhaps than having one's name on a building, but more impactful to advancing inclusion and reforming meritocracy.) Trustees interested in how well their universities are contributing to upward mobility overall will monitor statistics about matriculation and graduation of students who are in the first generation of their family to attend college. Those who are interested in racial diversity will monitor the same statistics for minority students. Those interested in socioeconomic diversity will monitor statistics about students on Pell Grants. All trustees should understand their university's commitment to avoiding a double standard in admissions. And leaders of the private sector who are trustees or members of visiting committees can enhance equal opportunity for enrolled students by providing mentoring, paid internships, and summer jobs.

In the current political environment, trustees should be alert to anti-DEI state legislation. For example, shortly before the decision came down in Harvard/UNC, Florida and Texas enacted bans on DEI offices in public colleges and universities.[18] In 2024, Alabama enacted legislation that prohibits DEI programs at "certain public entities" and that also prohibits "the promotion, endorsement, and affirmation of certain divisive concepts in public settings," including "that meritocracy or traits such as hard work are racist or sexist."[19] In fact, the Manhattan Institute, a think tank that describes its mission as being "to develop and disseminate new ideas that foster greater economic choice and individual responsibility," has published model legislation for use by states. That legislation is designed to "abolish DEI bureaucracies"; to "end mandatory diversity training"; to "curtail political coercion" that the authors assert results from the use of "so-called 'diversity statements'"; and to "end identity-based preferences" in admissions or employment.[20] The Iowa ban on DEI programs in its higher-education system contains an exception reading "except as provided by federal or state law or accreditation standards." The state legislator who introduced the bill has accused the medical school at the University of Iowa of improperly relying on the accreditation "loophole" to keep open its Office of Health Parity.[21]

Ohio had under consideration a bill that would, among other things, prohibit mandatory DEI training.[22] In response, the Inter-University Council of Ohio told the Ohio legislature that "data shows, DEI efforts help create an academic community that generates a higher enrollment rate, matriculation rate, and eventual success rate." It said further that "prohibiting all DEI also puts Ohio's students at a disadvantage in the workforce [because] many employers are looking for well-educated individuals who can perform in a diverse work environment."[23] Responding through an association rather than by individual schools was a savvy approach. The Ohio bill was withdrawn in December 2023.

As part of the federal attack on DEI beginning at the outset of the second Trump administration, on February 14, 2025, the Office for Civil Rights of the US Department of Education issued a "dear colleague" letter asserting, "Educational institutions have toxically indoctrinated students with the false premise that the United States is built upon 'systemic and structural racism' . . . [and] have attempted to further justify them . . . under the banner of [DEI]." The letter advised educational institutions, among other things, to "cease all efforts to circumvent prohibitions on the use of race" and warned that failing "to comply with federal civil rights law" could result in a loss of federal funding. This was a very different "dear colleague" message than the one referred to above!

The admission of students from a broad range of backgrounds is just a starting point for realizing the benefits of a diverse student body. One professor has urged that universities be urged to "make diversity an educational asset" by encouraging students of all backgrounds, and even those in the STEM disciplines, to engage in discussions of "the big questions posed by the humanities." This can be achieved through a so-called core curriculum or "general education" requirements.[24]

Two other professors make a related point. They argue that "intolerance of ideas," the hallmark of culture wars, "is not just a consequence of an increasingly polarized society." Rather "we think it also results from the failure of higher education to provide students with the kind of shared intellectual framework we call civic education."[25] Some employers are filling this gap with workplace seminars on civics and democracy designed to encourage more civil discourse among their employees.[26] Another caveat: Some advocacy of civic education has an ideological slant—with a focus on "patriotism, Christianity, and anti-communism."[27] And the decision of the board of the University of North Carolina to establish a School of Civic Life and Leadership was viewed by some on the university's faculty with skepticism ". . . alleging the new school to be some kind of right-wing Republican fifth column."[28]

It has been asserted that an absence of a broad-based education "has fueled a rampant vocationalism among students, leading them to desert humanities classes in favor of preprofessional tracks aimed at lucrative careers."[29] And a recent graduate of the University of Pennsylvania published an opinion piece under the headline "Careerism is Ruining College" and asserted that it is taking an "emotional toll" on students.[30] There is evidence supporting these assertions. In the Frank Bruni book discussed earlier, he cites statistics reported by William Deresiewicz in *Excellent Sheep* about the "grim ascendance of economics as a major—and finance and management consulting as careers—for a shocking percentage of young people who attend the most highly selective colleges." Deresiewicz reported, further, that "In 2011, more than a third of Princeton's graduates went into finance alone."[31] And, in a 2024 article in *The New York Times Magazine*, it was observed that "even when they arrive at college wanting something very different, an increasing number of students at elite universities seek the imprimatur of employment by a powerful firm and 'making a bag' (slang for a sack of money) as quickly as possible."[32]

There may be some positive news, however, in the statistics from the top-ranked business schools about the current interests of their graduates in recent years. On average only about one-third of those graduates are going into finance, roughly the same number as those going into consulting. But entrepreneurship has generated a great deal of interest. While only a single-digit percentage of graduates of most of those schools pursue starting their own business right after graduation, three years later the percentage has grown significantly. Interestingly, at Chicago Booth, long known for its reputation in finance, some 70 percent of current students are pursuing a concentration in entrepreneurship. Even if that interest is driven by a desire to make lots of money, at least it would be the result of "making something." And however the future elite in business makes lots of money, hopefully exposure to a broader education and exposure to a diverse group of fellow students will encourage them to be civic minded and generous philanthropists.

It is also the case that not all who are considered to be in the elite are among those seeking to maximize their compensation. The elite in medicine tend to gravitate to academic medical centers, the NIH, and the CDC and are compensated well below what private practice physicians and surgeons make. Many elite lawyers are also in academia or have joined the judiciary or the Department of Justice. Elite scientists work at universities, the national labs, NASA, and so on. Finally, there are the elite who are social entrepreneurs or otherwise work in the not-for-profit sector. Sometimes, this is a second career for those who made their money in business and finance.

Finally, in commentary following the Harvard/UNC cases, two academic sociologists make pretty compelling, data-driven points that (1) affirmative action at highly selective universities actually did very little in terms of moving the needle toward educational equity and that (2) a better approach would be a "collective recommitment to the quality and success of more accessible institutions," presumably through philanthropy and other means.[33] Consider, for example, the gifts by MacKenzie Scott to historically Black colleges and universities (HBCUs) and other institutions serving minorities that have reportedly exceeded $800 million, as well as the HBCU Transformation Project, which was funded by a $124 million gift from Blue Meridian Partners. Coupling that with greater resistance to credentialism, could be a formula for significant reform of meritocracy and revitalization of the American Dream. On the other hand, much like the caveat about not encouraging promising high-potential youth to settle for less than a four-year degree, they should also not be discouraged from aspiring to admission to selective colleges.

GOVERNMENT

For the reasons discussed in chapter 5, the private sector is better suited than government to reform meritocracy. Nevertheless, as noted in that discussion, there are issues largely within the purview of government that need to be attended to in order achieve equal opportunity for individuals to compete in a meritocracy. Leaders in the private sector should use their influence to encourage—indeed, insist—that elected and appointed governmental officials attend to those critical issues.

Moreover, before voting for, or making personal donations to, candidates for elective office, leaders in the private sector should assess the merits of the candidates in the same way they would consider the qualifications of a candidate for an important job in their organizations. As one commentator has correctly asserted, "democracy requires competence."[34]

Democracy also benefits from good character on the part of elected and appointed officials. FDR made this point when he said that the presidency "is preeminently a place of moral leadership."[35] And focusing on the current political environment, another commentator noted "nothing is more corrosive to a vibrant democracy and healthy communities . . . than 'when leaders with formal authority behave without moral authority.'"[36]

One of the strongest statements along these lines was made by the Southern Baptist Convention (SBC) in its 1998 "Resolution on Moral Character of Public Officials," adopted soon after the Clinton/Lewinsky scandal. That document was actually a series of resolutions and included the following: "we implore our government leaders to live by the highest standards of morality"; "tolerance of serious wrong by leaders sears the conscience of the culture"; "we urge all Americans to embrace and act on the conviction that character does count in public office, and to elect those officials and candidates who, although imperfect, demonstrate consistent honesty, moral purity, and the highest character."[37] (This admonition appears to have been ignored by many white evangelicals, given their voting patterns since 2016.[38] The rationale for evangelical support of Trump, despite his failure to meet the standards of the SBC resolution was explained by Tim Alberta as follows: "Trump was introduced [by evangelical leaders as] . . . the latest in a long line of flawed men who were being used by God to advance his purposes"; flawed men like King Cyrus, in the Bible.[39]) Nevertheless, insisting that our elected officials are highly competent and of good character will strengthen our democracy.

The need for citizens to consider the character of a candidate before voting for him or her in the election of a US president has become even more compelling in light of the 2024 SCOTUS decision in *Trump v. US*.[40] That decision held that a president has "absolute immunity" from criminal liability when taking official actions that fall within the exclusive presidential powers. It held, further, that there is "at least presumptive immunity" governing other official acts. It is only "unofficial acts"—"perhaps as a candidate for office or party leader"—for which there is no immunity. The delineation between and among these three categories, and thus full impact of this decision, remains to be worked out. The dissent of Justice Sotomayor may have incorrectly concluded that the decision would allow a president to act with impunity in the hypothetical about ordering SEAL Team Six to assassinate a political rival—but she might not be wrong. This decision on presidential immunity suggests that citizens will not be able to rely on the courts to corral a whole range of potentially criminal activity on the part of a president. Moreover, recent experiences with impeachments—those of Clinton and Trump in which acquittals were provided by the Senate seemingly on purely political bases—tell us that we cannot rely on that mechanism either for holding presidents accountable for misdeeds. And those concerns should be considered in the context that, in the view of Christopher DeMuth (a distinguished fellow at the Heritage Foundation), "the presidency has become much more powerful and less benign than it was designed to be."[41] Jefferson's emphasis on "virtue" has never been more important in the context of a presidential election.

In addition to having government officials of competence and good character, a well-operating democracy requires robust participation by the electorate. The private sector can play a role in encouraging voter participation by employees and even consumers, and efforts in that regard can be appropriate if based on a sense that it is good for business. Companies utilize a variety of strategies, including paid time off to allow employees to vote. All of this is described in a case study from the Ash Center at the Harvard Kennedy School.[42] And, leaders of the private sector who serve on university boards should consider the example set by Wesleyan University with its Democracy 2024 program. Among other things, that program will "provide grant opportunities to support students who want to work on campaigns around the country."[43]

Leaders of the private sector should insist that elected officials, when called upon to nominate or confirm individuals for *appointive* office apply the criteria that those in the private sector use (or, as advocated here, should use) in hiring and promoting their employees. And when elected officials support the appointment of unqualified individuals or stand in the way of the appointment of clearly qualified individuals, they should be held accountable. There have been regrettable examples of both of these last two points as they apply to federal judicial appointments. In the 1970s, Senator Roman Hruska was challenged about the nomination of Judge Carswell to the US Supreme Court. His memorable response: "Even if he [Carswell] were mediocre, there are a lot of mediocre judges and people and lawyers. They are entitled to a little representation, aren't they?"[44] And then there is the action by the Senate Majority Leader McConnell in refusing to advance the nomination of Merrick Garland to fill the vacancy created by the death of Justice Scalia.

Another thought, perhaps literally fantastic but a fun digression, would be for leaders in the private sector to demand that government officials adhere to the standards that apply to public company executives and boards. Start with the duty of care—Shouldn't a legislator be required to read and understand a bill before voting on it? Then how about requiring compliance with the duty of loyalty—not taking actions or voting for the sole purpose of retaining their seat. It would be wonderful to require compliance with the duties of candor that result from both fiduciary duty and the securities laws. Shouldn't résumé fraud and intentionally lying or recklessly making untrue statements to constituents be disqualifying?

Less fantastic would be to encourage governments to pursue meritocratic reform when they act as consumers and employers. As consumers, they could encourage vendor diversity and, also, entrepreneurship by buying from minority- and women-owned enterprises. On the other hand, some state and local governments may feel constrained by the aforementioned views of the state attorneys general. As employers, they could address credentialism, like a number of governments have done, by no longer requiring a four-year college diploma where a position does not actually require it.

COMMUNITIES

Leaders interested in enhancing equal opportunity, and thus reforming meritocracy and revitalizing the American Dream, through actions in the community might consider supporting one or more of a number of programs.

There are programs related to education. According to the National Education Association, early childhood education—pre-K and kindergarten—"give children the foundation they need for a lifetime of learning and success." Among other things, children who have had the benefit of such programs are more likely to graduate from high school.[45] Early childhood education is a near certainty in affluent areas; it is far less so in the inner city and rural areas. Public school programs that enhance equal opportunity include free breakfast and lunch (and should be provided in a manner that doesn't stigmatize the recipients), tutoring and after-school sports, art, and music. Careful thought should be given to whether or not to eliminate early "gifted students" programs or delay until after freshman year the start of high school honors programs (as discussed briefly in chapter 3).

Many companies participate in "adopt-a-school" programs—providing financial support and encouraging their employees to contribute time to reading, tutoring, coaching, and other programs that involve personal interactions with students. Those involved in such interactions can convey what may be the greatest gift of all—an expectation that the students can be successful. But that expectation may need to be backed up with long-term mentoring and additional forms of support.

In addition to supporting public education, many leaders in the private sector have influence with private schools. Recruiting and funding scholarships at those schools for students who would otherwise not be able to afford to attend could greatly enhance the diversity of those student bodies and enrich the educational experience for all students—importantly, "benefiting wealthier students who may have had little exposure to peers from other backgrounds."[46]

There are other ways that the private sector can invest time and money in their communities. Summer employment and sports, art, and music opportunities for inner-city and rural youth can benefit both the youth and contribute to reduction in crime and drug addiction. Other actions to consider include addressing inner-city food deserts, gun violence, affordable childcare, and supporting civil legal aid clinics. Finally, support can be provided to not-for-profits (including religious organizations) that endeavor to help families.

Perhaps the most potent, but most difficult, reform at the community level to achieve equal opportunity relates to affordable housing. Richard Kahlenberg, a policy consultant and academic, has written that, "since passage of the 1968 Fair Housing Act, racial segregation in housing has fallen by 30 percent but income segregation has doubled, in part because of pervasive class discrimination through zoning" and that "exclusionary housing practices are a linchpin in the architecture of educational inequality in America." Finally, he notes that "economic segregation of students . . . shapes educational opportunity even more powerfully than spending per pupil."[47] That said, it has been reported that there is a $23 billion school funding gap between majority white and majority non-white public school districts.[48] Another author has identified exclusionary zoning as breeding "among blue-collar whites a festering resentment toward elites."[49] Finally, when income or economic segregation results in "concentrated poverty," that concentration results in "diminished school quality and academic achievement; diminished health and healthcare quality; pervasive joblessness, employment discrimination, and reduced employment networks; increased crime, especially violent crime; declining and poorly maintained housing stock and devaluation of home values; and difficulty building wealth and experiencing economic mobility."[50] So, if leaders in the private sector are looking for a truly effective means for reforming meritocracy and revitalizing the American Dream beyond their own organizations, the fight against NIMBY may be the way to go.

When addressing issues in the community, leaders in the private sector may be more effective when they band together. A great example of this is the Commercial Club of Chicago, whose membership comprises the elite of the city's business and professional communities. The Club's Civic Committee has tackled issues such as public safety, business diversity, opportunities for veterans, affordable housing, and public education.

• • •

Leaders in the private sector can clearly reform meritocracy and revitalize the American Dream both inside and outside of their organizations. In the next chapter, we will briefly consider why they should.

III

WHY BOTHER?

10

A "TO-DO LIST" FOR REFORM

In the preface, I mentioned that after nearly a half century of advising CEOs and boards of directors, I know that there can be a limited appetite on the part of my target audience for lengthy discourse. That same experience, and my own work habits, make me a fan of "to-do lists." So, as a means of summarizing this book and to facilitate your helping to reform meritocracy and revitalize the American Dream, here is a list of actions, one or more of which you might consider taking:

1. Adopt a robust definition of merit—using the baseline definition in chapter 2 with additional elements appropriate to the specific context. When the time comes to select a successor CEO for any organization with which you are associated, make sure the winning candidate sincerely signs on to your definition of merit and, also, shares your commitment to meritocracy. That way, you can have more confidence that the new CEO will build a strong team.
2. Be diligent and self-aware when applying the definition of merit in making hiring and promoting decisions about others—that is, consider both unconscious and cognitive bias.
3. Ask yourself how well you comport with that robust definition, especially the part about humility, and make necessary adjustments. Remember that a humble leader will have more success in attracting and retaining followers. Moreover, hubris on the part of the elite adds to the appeal of demagogues.

4. If, after following an appropriate corporate governance process, you have concluded that having a diverse workforce and management group serves the long-term best interests of the corporation and its shareholders, do not be deterred from pursuing efforts—including a DEI program—designed to achieve that goal. Be prepared, however, to respond to pushback. And by all means, when pursuing diversity, firmly resist the application of a double standard.
5. Resist entreaties of individuals in your business and social networks seeking your help to bestow meritocratic inheritance (through jobs, college admissions, and other) when the proposed beneficiaries are not fully qualified or deserving.
6. Utilize at least part of your personal and organizational philanthropic activities (money and time) in service of reforming meritocracy—that is, consider whether those activities contribute to equal opportunity or whether they further meritocratic inheritance. Ditto, with respect to commenting or lobbying on public policy issues.
7. Be a mentor to someone who has high potential, but who comes from a background with few role models who can guide him or her toward success. Give that person the gift of high expectations.
8. Especially for those in your organization with high potential, address the potential for burnout. Don't let meritocracy be a trap for those folks.
9. Resist credentialism, but continue to encourage individuals with high potential to pursue a four-year college degree at the best school they can get into.
10. Create, or support existing, pipeline and apprenticeship programs.
11. Don't support, or vote for, politicians you would not want as colleagues in your organization. Among other things, support, and vote for, only politicians of high integrity. If more of the right folks get elected, maybe trust in government will be restored and the public sector can share with the private sector more of the task of reforming meritocracy and revitalizing the American Dream.

ACKNOWLEDGMENTS

The individuals I wish to acknowledge fall into two categories—those who, perhaps unknowingly on their part, introduced me and held my attention to the subject; and those who helped me create this book and make it better than I could have done on my own.

That first category is largely occupied by colleagues at the only law firm I was part of for nearly half a century. Howard Trienens and Newton Minow served as my mentors from shortly after the start of my career through my retirement. As firm leaders, they fostered meritocracy without ever articulating that as an explicit goal. Those two giants of the profession, more than anyone else at the firm, were responsible for the comment captured in the introduction about the firm being a near-perfect meritocracy. It was they who instigated and integrated the merger of an old-school WASP firm (old Sidley) with a somewhat smaller, largely Jewish firm (Liebman Williams) three years before I joined as an associate in 1975. It was they who brought on board the first Black partner in 1975. It was they who promoted the first woman partner to our executive committee. (They eschewed credentialism; she had not graduated from anything close to an elite law school.) It was they who promoted a part-time female associate to partnership. On a more personal level, it was they who gave me so many opportunities, despite a total absence on my part of any existing connection to clients or to their network. It was they who embodied, and modeled for me, so many of the elements of the robust definition of merit that appears elsewhere in this book.

Also in that first category are colleagues in firm management and the vast majority of our partners who embraced the need for us to expand the available pool of talent in our firm and, through our pipeline program, in the profession at large. They also recognized the importance of resisting a double standard—whether when pursuing diversity or considering the demands of clients and others who were seeking to facilitate meritocratic inheritance.

Last in that first category—with perhaps some irony—is Daniel Markovits. He is the Yale law professor (who I have never met nor spoken to) whose book, *The Meritocracy Trap*, I disagreed with so much that I felt compelled to write what is, in part, an "opposing brief."

Turning to the second category—those who helped so much with this book.

There are those who, upon hearing from me that I was thinking about writing this book, provided some suggestions and cautions, as well as words of encouragement and support. For example, one person said, "So, you want to dive right into the culture wars?" Another said, "You can't write about that without addressing race." A third said, "You must write that book, and be sure you cover 'credentialism.'" (I immediately nodded, but had to look up what that meant.)

Also in this second category is my unpaid, but hardworking, panel of private reviewers. There were three who commented extensively on numerous drafts: Paul Hennessy (a retired senior banker at JPMorgan); Peter Keisler (my now-retired partner of many years who also served as the acting attorney general of the United States during the George W. Bush administration); Aric Press (the former editor-in-chief of *The American Lawyer*). I am most grateful to them for their insightful comments and the hours they spent going over my manuscript. And then there are two members of my family, Connie (my wife) and Emily (my lawyer-turned-entrepreneur daughter), who provided valuable substantive and editorial suggestions.

This book would clearly not have been published but for the support and expertise of my editor at the University of Chicago Press, Chad Zimmerman. We worked together on this project for over three years. His provocative questions and thoughtful suggestions made this a much, much better book. And he organized the Press's rigorous vetting process—anonymous reviewers and committees—that every author should want to be subjected to. The Press also got me in touch with Laura Tsitlidze, a copyeditor extraordinaire.

Finally, thanks to my long-standing assistant, Cathy Chow. She very patiently and expertly helped generate dozens of drafts of the manuscript.

While many folks—those named and others unnamed—provided great advice and inspiration, I acknowledge that I am solely responsible for the contents of this book and the positions espoused herein.

APPENDIX A
BOOKS ABOUT MERITOCRACY

As noted in the preface, there has been a deluge of books about meritocracy, some of which are quite recent, but none of which were published after the US Supreme Court decision in the Harvard/UNC cases. Some of the books are about meritocracy as a general matter. Others are about meritocracy in higher education. The books listed in this appendix are presented in alphabetical order by author. All of the authors are either academics or journalists. Quotations from the books (mostly from their introductions) are designed to provide a fair summary, in the words of the authors, of their main theses. Some of those quotations echo the positions taken in this book; others (e.g., from the Giridharadas book) reflect a very different perspective. Some of the other authors are not fans of the concept, even if reformed.

Carnevale, Anthony P., Peter Schmidt, and Jeff Strohl. *The Merit Myth: How Our Colleges Favor the Rich and Divide America*. The New Press, 2020.

- “Using selective colleges as gatekeepers, [the] elite has shut large swaths of the American population out of having access to power, opportunity, and wealth. . . . In the modern republic, colleges should do more than groom successive generations of governing elites” (3).

- "On the whole, higher education serves to compound the advantages or disadvantages that people had as children" (7).
- "More than two hundred years [after the founding of the republic], we're told that higher education produces a meritocracy. . . . Not true. Even as higher education has become more widely accessible, especially in recent decades, it has also become much more widely stratified by class and race" (13).
- "Partly as a result of . . . practices within higher education, our society is becoming a meritocracy in name only. . . . The ideal of meritocracy assumes that the elite will be churned by social mobility, that people will rise into the elite through high performance or fall out of it from failure. In reality, our education system helps cement our elite into place, ensuring families' perpetuation of their favored status from one generation to the next" (15).
- "We've seen signs in recent years that at least some presidents of selective colleges are giving greater weigh to considerations of opportunity" (18). "It seems unlikely, however, that most selective or somewhat selective American colleges will reform themselves without being guided, coaxed, and prodded" (19).
- "We seek to rebalance our educational system's role as both a rewarder of merit and a provider of equal opportunity" (25).

Frank, Robert H. *Success and Luck: Good Fortune and the Myth of Meritocracy*. Princeton University Press, 2016.

- "As a practical matter . . . no system could ever be perfectly meritocratic" (xii).
- "I believe the rhetoric of meritocracy has caused enormous harm. . . . [it] appears to have camouflaged the extent to which success and failure often hinge decisively on events completely beyond an individual's control" (xii).
- "There are of course many people who are quick to acknowledge good fortune's contribution to their success. Those people, it turns out, are much more likely than others to support the kinds

of public investments that created and maintained the environments that made their own success possible" (xvi).

Giridharadas, Anand. *Winners Take All: The Elite Charade of Changing the World*. Knopf, 2018.

- "Many millions of Americans, on the Left and Right, feel one thing in common: that the game is rigged against people like them" (4).
- "All around us, the winners in our highly inequitable status quo declare themselves partisans of change. . . . The initiatives [they propose] mostly aren't democratic . . . they favor the use of the private sector and its charitable spoils, the market way of looking at things, and the bypassing of government" (5).
- "This book is an attempt to understand the connection between these elites' social concern and predation" (7).
- "Private and voluntary half-measures . . . crowd out public solutions that would solve problems for everyone . . . when elites assume leadership of social change, they are able to reshape what social change is—above all, to present it as something that should never threaten winners" (8).

  "What is at stake is whether the reform of our common life is led by governments elected by and accountable to the people, or rather by wealthy elites claiming to know our best interests" (10).

Guinier, Lani. *The Tyranny of the Meritocracy: Democratizing Higher Education in America*. Beacon Press, 2015.

- "The testocracy, a twenty-first-century cult of standardized, quantifiable merit, values perfect scores but ignores character" (ix).
- "We need to reexamine exactly how we define 'merit'" (xi).
- "Democratic merit . . . provides educational access to those who serve the goals and contribute to the conditions of a thriving

democracy . . . it creates an incentive system that emphasizes not just the possession of individual talent . . . but also the ability to collaborate and the commitment to building a better society for more people" (xiii).

Hayes, Christopher. *Twilight of the Elites: America After Meritocracy*. Broadway, 2012.

- "Like all ruling orders, the meritocracy tends to cultivate within its most privileged members and abiding devotion" (20).
- "Recruitment into the top ranks of the meritocracy also cultivates a disposition to trust one's fellow meritocrats. . . . In place of the old WASP establishment, America embraced meritocracy" (21).
- "In reality our meritocracy has failed not because it is too meritocratic, but because in practice, it isn't very meritocratic at all" (53).

Kirn, Walter. *Lost in the Meritocracy: The Undereducation of an Overachiever*. Anchor, 2009.

- "Percentile [on the SAT] is destiny in America" (5).
- "A natural-born child of the meritocracy, I'd ben amassing momentum my whole life. . . . Learning was secondary, promotion was primary" (9).
- "A pure meritocracy . . . can only promote; it can't legitimize. It can confer success but can't grant knighthood. For that it needs a class beyond itself: the high-born genealogical peerage that aptitude testing was created to overthrow" (171).

Littler, Jo. *Against Meritocracy: Culture, Power and Myths of Mobility*. Routledge, 2018.

- "This book argues that it is not merely a coincidence that a pronounced lack of social mobility and the continual importance of inherited wealth [citations omitted] coexist with the common idea that we live in a meritocratic age. On the contrary: the idea of meritocracy has become a key means through with plutocracy—or government by a wealthy elite—perpetuates, reproduces, and extends itself. Meritocracy has become the key means of cultural legitimation for contemporary capitalist culture.... The language of meritocracy has become an alibi for plutocracy" (2).

- "Meritocracy offers a ladder system of social mobility, promoting a corrosive ethic of competitive self-interest which both legitimizes inequality and damages community" (3).
- "The emphasis on effort is the element of meritocracy that has been expanded in recent years" (7).

Markovits, Daniel. *The Meritocracy Trap: How America's Foundational Myth Feeds Inequality, Dismantles the Middle Class, and Devours the Elite*. Penguin Press, 2019.

- "Meritocracy entices an anxious and inauthentic elite into a pitiless, lifelong contest to secure income and status through its own excessive industry" (x).
- "Meritocracy . . . did open up the elite in its early years, it now more nearly stifles than fosters social mobility" (xiv).
- "Emancipation [from meritocracy] would invite the elite, now entangled in strained self-exploitation, to trade diminution in wealth and status that it can easily afford in exchange for a precious increase in leisure and liberty, a reclaiming of an authentic self" (xxii).
- "Meritocracy has become the single greatest obstacle to equal opportunity in America today" (27).
- "Meritocratic inheritance now drives a wedge between meritocracy and opportunity" (147).

McNamee, Stephen J. *The Meritocracy Myth*. 4th ed. Rowman & Littlefield, 2018.

- “The presumption that the system [of meritocracy] as a whole fundamentally operates on the basis of merit in determining who gets what and how much is a myth” (ix).
- “A variety of non-merit factors, including inheritance, social and cultural capital, differential access to educational opportunities, reduced rates of self-employment, luck, and discrimination . . . tend to neutralize, suppress, or even negate the effects of individual merit” (ix).
- “Discrimination is the antithesis of merit. Where there is discrimination, there is no meritocracy” (16).
- “Besides education, the other most historically significant pathway for upward social mobility in America has been through some form of entrepreneurial activity . . . entrepreneurship [has a] . . . central place in the American Dream” (16).

Sandel, Michael J. *The Tyranny of Merit: Can We Find the Common Good?* Picador, 2020.

- “The problem with meritocracy is not with the principle but with our failure to live up to it” (11).
- “At a time when anger against the elites has brought democracy to the brink, the question of merit takes on a special urgency. We need to ask whether the solution to our fractious politics is to live more faithfully by the principle of merit, or to seek a common good beyond the sorting and the striving” (15).
- “Meritocratic hubris reflects the tendency of winners to inhale too deeply of their success, to forget the luck and good fortune that helped them on their way” (25).
- “There is reason to doubt that even a perfectly realized meritocracy would be a just society. To begin with . . . the meritocratic

ideal is about mobility, not equality. . . . The meritocratic ideal is not a remedy for inequality; it is a justification of inequality" (122).

- The "aristocracy of inherited privilege has given way to a meritocratic elite that is now as privileged and entrenched as the one it replaced" (166).

Wooldridge, Adrian. *The Aristocracy of Talent: How Meritocracy Made the Modern World*. Skyhorse Publishing, 2021.

- "Some of the sharpest critics of meritocracy come from the very heart of the meritocratic system itself. . . . The Markovits–Sandel fusillade is the latest example of the 'revolt of the elites' against the very ideology that is the foundation of their elite position" (6–7).
- "Is there a better system for organizing the world?" (9).
- "Many of today's sternest critics of meritocracy think it is beyond reform" (17).
- "Today's critics of the meritocratic idea nevertheless get one big thing right: that the meritocratic elite is in danger of hardening into an aristocracy which passes on its privileges to its children by investing heavily in education, and which, because of its sustained success, looks down on the rest of society" (17).

APPENDIX B
MATERIALS ABOUT DEI PROGRAMS

An internet search about DEI programs yields a seemingly endless number of items. Set forth in this appendix, organized by category, are some examples.

ARTICLES AND SERVICES FROM CONSULTING FIRMS

McKinsey & Company. "What Is Diversity, Equity, and Inclusion?," August 17, 2022. https://www.mckinsey.com/featured-insights/mckinsey-explainers/what-is-diversity-equity-and-inclusion. The article includes "five action areas" to be considered by "companies looking to step up their DEI efforts." It also links a number of its influential prior studies on the business benefits of diversity.

Boston Consulting Group. "Diversity, Equity, and Inclusion," https://www.bcg.com/capabilities/diversity-inclusion/overview. The firm describes its various consulting services in which they help "organizations rethink and broaden their DEI strategy from a 'do good' requirement to a lever for lasting competitive advantage, business opportunity, and societal change."

Qooper. "DEI Initiative Examples to Implement in 2023," https://www.qooper.io/blog/dei-initiative-examples. In a blog post (revised for 2024), this firm includes links to its training and leadership development programs.

Workhuman. "The Why Behind DE&I Initiatives: Examples, Benefits, Definition, and More," https://www.workhuman.com/blog/dei-initiatives/. This article includes steps for "creating a DEI initiative" and gives examples of the "top DE&I initiatives."

ACADEMIC PROGRAMS

Harvard Business School Online. "What Is DEI? Understanding Diversity, Equity, and Inclusion," October 3, 2023, https://online.hbs.edu/blog/post/what-is-dei. Michael Boyles provides "four tips for implementing DEI effectively" and promotes an online course entitled "Leadership, Ethics, and Corporate Accountability."

Harvard University Division of Continuing Education. "Equity, Diversity, Inclusion, and Belonging Leadership Graduate Certificate," https://extension.harvard.edu/academics/programs/equity-diversity-inclusion-and-belonging-leadership-graduate-certificate/. The Harvard extension school now offers an EDIB Leadership graduate certificate.

University of Michigan Rackham Graduate School. "Rackham Professional Development Diversity, Equity, and Inclusion Certificate," https://rackham.umich.edu/professional-development/dei-certificate/. The school offers a professional development certificate.

University of Pennsylvania Wharton School. "MBA Diversity, Equity & Inclusion (DEI) Major," https://mgmt.wharton.upenn.edu/programs/mba/dei-major/. The management department at Wharton began offering a management major in DEI in the 2023–24 academic year.

Brown University School of Professional Studies. "Applied Inclusive Leadership Certificate," https://professional.brown.edu/certificate/applieddei. The school offers an "applied inclusive leadership certificate."

ARTICLES LISTING "TOP" DEI PROGRAMS

Baragwanath, Tom. "13 Diversity Training Programs to Kickstart DEI in 2022." 360 Learning. https://360learning.com/blog/diversity-training-programs/.

Human Rights Careers. "10 Top-Rated Courses to Foster Diversity, Equity, and Inclusion (DEI)," https://www.humanrightscareers.com/magazine/dei-courses-online/.

APPENDIX C
CHRONOLOGY OF THE SHAREHOLDER VERSUS STAKEHOLDER DEBATE

Threshold question, the answer to which impacts how governance is structured and executed on: For whose *benefit* are decisions to be made? This is the subject of an ongoing debate (shorthand is "shareholders versus stakeholders"). Prevailing positions have ebbed and flowed over time, no doubt affected by then current economic trends and events.

1919—*Dodge v. Ford*—"It is not within the lawful power of a board of directors to shape and conduct the affairs of a corporation for the merely incidental benefit of shareholders and for the primary purpose of benefiting others . . ."

1932—Dodd-Berle Debate in *Harvard Law Review*—Against the backdrop of the crash of 1929 and the Great Depression, Professor Berle argued that corporate powers should be used only for the benefit of shareholders. Professor Dodd argues against "the view that business corporations exist for the sole purpose of making profits for their stockholders."

1953—"Corporate social responsibility" (CSR) term was coined by an American economist; usage of that term became much more common in the 1990s; near synonyms are "socially responsible investing" (SRI) and "environmental, social, and governance" (ESG).

1970—Milton Friedman's famous *New York Times Magazine* essay entitled "The Social Responsibility of Business Is to Increase Its Profits."

1973—Davos Manifesto—"The purpose of professional management is to serve clients, shareholders, workers, and employees, as well as societies, and to harmonize the different interests of the stakeholders."

1978—Control Data Corporation certificate of incorporation "other constituencies" provision. ("Other constituencies" are the non-shareholder stakeholders—employees, creditors, customers, suppliers, and communities.)

1981—Business Roundtable Statement of Corporate Responsibility: A corporation "must be a thoughtful institution which rises above the bottom line to consider the impact of its actions on all, from shareholders to the society at large."

1985—Revlon opinion by the Delaware Supreme Court; short version is that in deciding about a change in control, a board cannot consider the interests of the other constituencies.

Post-Revlon—Adoption of state "other constituencies" statutes (permissive or mandatory).

1992—Chancellor William Allen's essay entitled "Our Schizophrenic Conception . . ."—In this essay, Allen (the most influential corporate law jurist of his time) described two conflicting legal conceptions of the corporation: property and social entity. He concluded that the social entity conception had prevailed, because boards and managements could make decisions that benefited non-shareholders so long as they "act in pursuit of some vision of the corporation's long-term welfare [and they] may take action that precludes shareholders from accepting an immediate high-premium offer for their shares."

1997—Business Roundtable Statement on Corporate Governance: "The principal objective of a business enterprise is to generate economic returns to its owners."

2007—First "public benefit corporation" (a.k.a. "B Corp.") statutes enacted.

2013—Trados opinion by the Delaware Chancery Court: "When exercising their statutory responsibility, the standard of conduct requires that directors seek 'to promote the value of the corporation for the benefit of its stockholders.' 'It is, of course, accepted that a corporation may take steps, such as giving charitable contributions or paying higher wages, that do not maximize profits currently. They may do so, however, because such activities are rationalized as producing greater profits over the long term.'"

2013—Drucker Institute company rankings began, including social responsibility as a factor; has become *The Wall Street Journal*'s Management Top 250.

2018—BlackRock letter to CEOs: "Society is increasingly turning to the private sector and asking that companies respond to broader social challenges. Companies must benefit all of their stakeholders, including shareholders, employees, customers, and the communities in which they operate."

2019—Business Roundtable Statement on the Purposes of a Corporation: "a fundamental commitment to all stakeholders."

2020—ESG mutual funds exceeded $1 trillion of assets under management for the first time (in 1994, they held $1.9 billion).

2023—US Supreme Court decision in Harvard/UNC case leads to a turbocharged assault on DEI programs in corporate America.

NOTES

PREFACE

1 Cartoon included in Robert Mankoff, "What Cartoons Can Do," *New Yorker*, August 7, 2014.

INTRODUCTION

1 "Meritocracy," in *Merriam-Webster Dictionary*, https://www.merriam-webster.com/dictionary/meritocracy.
2 "Meritocracy," in *Cambridge Dictionary*, https://dictionary.cambridge.org/dictionary/english/meritocracy.
3 James Truslow Adams, *The Epic of America* (Simon Publications, 2001), 404.
4 Jon Meacham, *And Then There Was Light: Abraham Lincoln and the American Struggle* (Random House, 2022), xxxiii.
5 Martin Luther King Jr., "I Have a Dream," August 28, 1963, *NPR*, transcript, https://www.npr.org/2010/01/18/122701268/i-have-a-dream-speech-in-its-entirety.
6 Alan Fox, "Class and Equality," *Socialist Commentary* (May 1956): 13.
7 Michael Young, *The Rise of the Meritocracy*, new introduction by the author (Routledge, 2017), xii.
8 Todd Zywicki, "Rent-Seeking, Crony Capitalism, and the Crony Constitution," *Supreme Court Economic Review* 23, no. 1 (2015): 77–103. https://doi.org/10.1086/686473.
9 Ben Cohen and Robert O'Connell, "$100 Million a Year and Worth Every Penny," *Wall Street Journal*, June 8–9, 2024, B1.

10 Barbara Kingsolver, *Demon Copperhead* (Harper Perennial, 2024), 69.
11 John H. Cochrane, "Incompetent Elites Make Trump Look Appealing," *Wall Street Journal*, February 2, 2024.
12 Nelson D. Schwartz, *The Velvet Rope Economy: How Inequality Became Big Business* (Doubleday, 2020).
13 David Brooks, "My Unsettling Interview with Steve Bannon." *New York Times*, July 1, 2024.
14 William A. Galston, "A Left-Right Revolt Against the New Elites," *Wall Street Journal*, January 12, 2022, A15.
15 Michael J. Sandel, *The Tyranny of Merit: Can We Find the Common Good?* (Picador, 2020); Lani Guinier, *The Tyranny of the Meritocracy: Democratizing Higher Education in America* (Beacon Press, 2015).
16 Anthony P. Carnevale, Peter Schmidt, and Jeff Strohl, *The Merit Myth: How Our Colleges Favor the Rich and Divide America* (The New Press, 2020); Stephen J. McNamee, *The Meritocracy Myth*, 4th ed. (Rowman & Littlefield, 2018).
17 Christopher Hayes, *Twilight of the Elites: America After Meritocracy* (Broadway, 2012), 138.
18 Anand Giridharadas, *Winners Take All: The Elite Charade of Changing the World* (Knopf, 2018).
19 Daniel Markovits, *The Meritocracy Trap: How America's Foundational Myth Feeds Inequality, Dismantles the Middle Class, and Devours the Elite* (Penguin Press, 2019).
20 Jo Littler, *Against Meritocracy: Culture, Power and Myths of Mobility* (Routledge, 2018), 2.
21 Littler, *Against Meritocracy*, 7.
22 Littler, *Against Meritocracy*, 3.
23 David Brooks, *The Road to Character* (Random House, 2015), 254–55.
24 Littler, *Against Meritocracy*, 15.
25 Sandel, *Tyranny of Merit*, 122.
26 Alissa Quart, *Bootstrapped: Liberating Ourselves from the American Dream* (Harper Collins, 2023).
27 Jessica Sager, "125 George Carlin Quotes to Make You Laugh, Smile and Think," Parade.com, January 11, 2024, 26.
28 David Leonhardt, *Ours Was a Shining Future: The Story of the American Dream* (Random House, 2023), xxvii.
29 Nicholas Kristof, "The One Privilege Liberals Ignore," *New York Times*, September 14, 2023, A24.
30 Jon Meacham, *His Truth Is Marching On: John Lewis and the Power of Hope* (Random House, 2021), 207.
31 Katie Roiphe, "Teens Need Real Jobs, Not Elite Internship," *Wall Street Journal*, September 13, 2024.

CHAPTER ONE

1 Plato, *The Republic* (Penguin Classics, 2007).
2 Mark Cartwright, "The Civil Service Examinations of Imperial China," in *World History Encyclopedia* (2019).
3 "Thomas Jefferson to John Adams," October 28, 1813, in *The Founders' Constitution*, vol. 1, chap. 15, doc. 61 (University of Chicago Press), http://press-pubs.uchicago.edu/founders/documents/v1ch15s61.html.
4 "Thomas Jefferson to John Adams," *Founders' Constitution.*
5 Jon Meacham, *And Then There Was Light: Abraham Lincoln and the American Struggle* (Random House, 2022), xxix.
6 Plessy v. Ferguson, 163 U.S. 537 (1986).
7 National Archives, "Pendleton Act (1883)," *Milestone Documents*, https://www.archives.gov/milestone-documents/pendleton-act.
8 Ed Rampell, "The Birth of a Nation, the Most Racist Movie Ever Made," *Washington Post*, March 3, 2015.
9 Timothy Egan, *Fever in the Heartland* (Viking, 2023).
10 Doug Melville, *Invisible Generals: Rediscovering Family Legacy, and a Quest to Honor America's First Black Generals* (Black Privilege Publishing, 2023), 31; referencing the Army War College Report (1925), available at https://cafriseabove.org.
11 Centers for Disease Control, "The U.S. Public Health Service Untreated Syphilis Study at Tuskegee," accessed December 5, 2022, https://www.cdc.gov/tuskegee.
12 Fareed Zakaria, *Age of Revolutions: Progress and Backlash from 1600 to the Present* (Norton, 2024), 240.
13 Ronald J. Daniels, Grant Shreve, and Phillip Spector, *What Universities Owe Democracy* (Johns Hopkins, 2021), 52.
14 Daniels, Shreve, and Spector, *What Universities Owe Democracy*, 53–54.
15 Advertisement, *New York Times Magazine*, September 10, 2023, back cover.
16 Alan Greenspan and Adrian Wooldridge, *Capitalism in America: An Economic History of the United States* (Penguin Books, 2018), 282.
17 Daniels, Shreve, and Spector, *What Universities Owe Democracy*, 54.
18 Tom Brokaw, *The Greatest Generation* (Random House, 1998), xix.
19 Buzz Bissinger, *The Mosquito Bowl: A Game of Life and Death in World War II* (Harper Perennial, 2022), 1.
20 Robert J. Samuelson, *The Good Life and Its Discontents: The American Dream in the Age of Entitlement 1945–1995* (Times Books, 1995), xv.
21 Samuelson, *Good Life and Its Discontents.*

22 Elaine Tyler May, interviewed in "Women and Work," from the *American Experience* film *Tupperware*, PBS, https://www.pbs.org/wgbh/americanexperience/features/tupperware-may/.

23 Brown v. Board of Education of Topeka, 347 U.S. 483 (1954).

24 Theodore D. Segal, *Point of Reckoning: The Fight for Racial Justice at Duke University* (Duke University Press, 2021).

25 Will Elsbury, *Racial, Ethnic, and Religious Minorities in the Vietnam War: A Resource Guide* (Library of Congress, 2022); Christian G. Appy, *Working-Class War: American Combat Soldiers and Vietnam* (University of North Carolina Press, 1993).

26 Claire Cain Miller, "New SAT Data Highlights the Deep Inequality at the Heart of American Education," *New York Times*, October 23, 2023.

27 College Board, "Landscape Data and Methodology Summary," 2019, https://cb.org/landscape.

28 Daniels, Shreve, and Spector, *What Universities Owe Democracy*, 67.

29 Stu Schmill, "We Are Reinstating SAT/ACT Requirements for Future Admissions Cycles," MIT Admissions, March 28, 2022, https://mitadmissions.org/blogs/entry/we-are-reinstating-sat-act-requirements-for-future-admissions-cycles/.

30 Ross Douthat, "Can the Meritocracy Survive Without the SAT?," *New York Times*, April 29, 2023.

31 Ira Stoll, "Medical Schools Bail on Academic Merit and Intellectual Rigor," *Wall Street Journal*, January 30, 2023, A17.

32 Ivy Coach, "Fees of College Consultants," February 28, 2023, https://www.ivycoach.com/the-ivy-coach-blog/college-admissions/fees-college-consultants/.

33 Top Tier Admissions, "College Admissions Counseling," August 26, 2024, https://toptieradmissions.com/.

34 Caitlin Moscatello, "Inventing the Perfect College Applicant," *New York Magazine*, March 1–4, 2021.

35 Douglas Belkin, "The Guru Saying He Can Get Your 11-Year-Old into Harvard," *Wall Street Journal*, October 17, 2024.

36 Daniel Golden, "Many Colleges Bend Rules to Admit Rich Applicants: Seeking Big Donors, Duke Woos Beneficent 'Development Admits,'" *Wall Street Journal*, February 20, 2003.

37 Douglas Belkin, "Suit Shows Glide Path to Top Schools for Rich," *Wall Street Journal*, December 18, 2024, A1.

38 Michael J. Sandel, *The Tyranny of Merit: Can We Find the Common Good?* (Picador, 2020), 4.

39 Jason Zweig, "Charlie Munger's Life Was About Way More than Money," *Wall Street Journal*, November 29, 2023.

40 Quoted in Allison Schrager, "'The Accidental Equalizer' Review: The Luck of the Job," *Wall Street Journal*, November 28, 2023.

CHAPTER TWO

1 Amartya Sen, "Merit and Justice," chap. 1 in *Meritocracy and Economic Inequality*, ed. Kenneth Arrow, Samuel Bowles, and Steven N. Durlauf (Princeton University Press, 2000), 5.

2 Marcel Schwantes, "Warren Buffett Says Integrity Is the Most Important Trait to Hire For," InteCor International, https://www.intecorint.com/warren-buffett-integrity.html.

3 Regents of the University of California v. Bakke, 438 U.S. 265 (1978), 317.

4 Yuval Noah Harari, *Sapiens: A Brief History of Humankind* (Harper Perennial, 2015), 113.

5 Cleveland Clinic, "Cognitive Bias 101: What It Is and How to Overcome It," May 2, 2023, https://health.clevelandclinic.org/cognitive-bias.

6 Phaedra Boinodiris and Rebecca James, "Can AI Enhance Meritocracy Within the Workplace?," Cognitive World, April 28, 2020, https://cognitiveworld.com/articles/2020/4/28/can-ai-enhance-meritocracy-within-the-workplace.

7 Rohit Chopra, Kristen Clarke, Charlotte A. Burrows, and Lina M. Khan, Joint Statement on Enforcement Efforts Against Discrimination and Bias in Automated Systems, 2023, https://www.ftc.gov/system/files/ftc_gov/pdf/EEOC-CRT-FTC-CFPB-AI-Joint-Statement%28final%29.pdf.

8 American Association of University Professors, "Tenure," https://www.aaup.org/issues/tenure.

9 Marc Stein, "The End of Faculty Tenure and the Transformation of Higher Education," *Academe*, 2023, https://www.aaup.org/article/end-faculty-tenure-and-transformation-higher-education.

10 "Thomas Jefferson to John Adams," October 28, 1813, in *The Founders' Constitution*, vol. 1, chap. 15, doc. 61 (University of Chicago Press).

11 Phillip Bump, "With Six Words, Michelle Obama Rewires America's Conversation on Race," *Washington Post*, August 21, 2024.

12 Stephen J. McNamee, *The Meritocracy Myth*, 4th ed. (Rowman & Littlefield, 2018), ix.

13 Raj Chetty, David J. Deming, and John N. Friedman, "Diversifying Society's Leaders? The Determinants and Causal Effects of Admission to Highly Selective Private Colleges," *National Bureau*

of Economic Research Working Paper No. 31492, July 2023, https://opportunityinsights.org/paper/collegeadmissions/.

14 "Credentialism," in *New Oxford American Dictionary*.

15 Michael J. Sandel, *The Tyranny of Merit: Can We Find the Common Good?* (Picador, 2020), 81, 104.

16 Jennifer Breheny Wallace, *Never Enough: When Achievement Culture Becomes Toxic* (Portfolio, 2023).

17 Cartoon included in Robert Mankoff, "What Cartoons Can Do," *New Yorker*, August 7, 2014.

18 Emily Bobrow, "David Novak," *Wall Street Journal*, March 12–13, 2022, C6.

19 Callum Borchers, "Successful Bosses Love Talking About Their Fast-Food Jobs," *Wall Street Journal*, October 14, 2024.

20 Rachel Shin, "A Professor Has Tracked the Colleges of Fortune 500 CEOs for 20 Years. He Was Stunned to Learn Ivy Leagues Don't Matter That Much," *Fortune*, June 14, 2023, https://fortune.com/2023/06/14/fortune-500-ceo-colleges-ivy-league/.

21 Frank Bruni, "The Unsung Alma Maters," chap.1 in *Where You Go Is Not Who You'll Be: An Antidote to the College Admissions Mania* (Grand Central Publishing, 2016).

22 Sherin Shibu, "Grads from This Midwestern School Are More Likely to Start a Billion Dollar Company than Founders Who Went to Stanford, Harvard, or MIT: Study," *Entrepreneur*, February 24, 2024, https://www.entrepreneur.com/business-news/a-midwest-college-is-most-likely-to-produce-unicorn-founders/470419.

23 Pamela Paul, "The Republican Party's Elite Conundrum," *New York Times*, July 25, 2024.

24 James Davison Hunter, *Culture Wars: The Struggle to Define America* (Basic Books, 1991).

25 Hunter, *Culture Wars*, 48–49.

26 John Freund, "Are You 'Woke'? Should You Be?," *Vincentian Mindwalk*, November 17, 2023.

27 Ron DeSantis, "Why I Stood Up to Disney," *Wall Street Journal*, March 1, 2023, A17.

28 Vivek Ramaswamy, "Why I'm Running for President," *Wall Street Journal*, February 22, 2023, A15.

29 "Upward Mobility," in *Merriam-Webster Dictionary*, https://www.merriam-webster.com/dictionary/upward%20mobility.

30 Aleyna Rentz, "Journalist David Leonhardt Discusses the Decline of the American Dream," The Hub, November 9, 2023, https://hub.jhu.edu/2023/11/09/authors-and-insights-david-leonhardt/; Sandel, *Tyranny of Merit*, 75.

31 Bruni, "Unsung Alma Maters," 131.

32 Raj Chetty, Will S. Dobbie, Benjamin Goldman, Sonya Porter, and Crystal Yang, "Changing Opportunity: Sociological Mechanisms Underlying Growing Class Gaps and Shrinking Race Gaps in Economic Mobility," *National Bureau of Economic Research Working Paper* No. 32697, July 2024, https://opportunityinsights.org/paper/changingopportunity/.

33 Bernie Marcus, "Entrepreneurship Will Lift Minorities Up," *Wall Street Journal*, January 10, 2023, A15.

34 Dean Struyven, Gizelle George-Joseph, and Daniel Milo, *Black Womenomics: Investing in the Underinvested*, Goldman Sachs Research, March 9, 2021, https://www.goldmansachs.com/pdfs/insights/pages/black-womenomics-f/black-womenomics-report.pdf.

35 American Alliance for Equal Rights v. Fearless Fund Management, LLC et al. (11th Cir. June 3, 2024).

CHAPTER THREE

1 The Annie E. Casey Foundation, "What's the Difference Between Equity and Equality?," November 20, 2023, https://www.aecf.org/blog/equity-vs-equality.

2 Yuval Noah Harari, *Sapiens: A Brief History of Humankind* (Harper Perennial, 2015), 164.

3 Amartya Sen, "Merit and Justice," chap. 1 in *Meritocracy and Economic Inequality*, ed. Kenneth Arrow, Samuel Bowles, and Steven N. Durlauf (Princeton University Press, 2000), 14.

4 Fareed Zakaria, *Age of Revolutions: Progress and Backlash from 1600 to the Present* (Norton, 2024), 10.

5 N. Derek Brown, Drew S. Jacoby-Senghor, and Isaac Raymundo, "If You Rise, I Fall: Equality Is Prevented by the Misperception That It Harms Advantaged Groups," *Science Advances* 8, no. 18 (May 6, 2020).

6 Troy Closson, "Court Allows Case Challenging Segregation in N.Y.C. Schools to Advance," *New York Times*, May 2, 2024.

7 Jillian Jorgensen, "This Brooklyn School Is Already Phasing Out 'Gifted and Talented' Classes," Spectrum News NY1, October 11, 2021.

8 Sara Randazzo, "Schools Cut Honors Classes to Address Racial Equity. It Isn't a Quick Fix," *Wall Street Journal*, October 9, 2023.

9 Joe Feagin and Zinobia Bennefeld, "Systemic Racism and U.S. Health Care," *Social Science & Medicine* 103 (2014), https://doi.org/10.1016/j.socscimed.2013.09.006.

10 Latoya Hill and Samantha Artiga, "What Is Driving Widening Racial Disparities in Life Expectancy?," *KFF*, May 23, 2023.
11 Donna L. Hoyert, *Maternal Mortality Rates in the United States, 2021*, National Center for Health Statistics, Center for Disease Control and Prevention, March 2023; American Society of Anesthesiologists, "Systemic Racism Plays Role in Much Higher Maternal Mortality Rate Among Black Women," press release, October 22, 2022.
12 Michelle Alexander, *The New Jim Crow*, 10th Anniversary Edition (The New Press, 2020), xvi.
13 Isabel Wilkerson, *Caste: The Origins of Our Discontents* (Random House, 2023) 17, 19.
14 Federal Reserve Bank of Kansas City, "Community Reinvestment Act of 1977," May 8, 2023, *Federal Reserve History*, https://www.federalreservehistory.org.
15 Richard Rothstein, *The Color of Law: A Forgotten History of How Our Government Segregated America* (Liveright, 2017), xvii.
16 US Department of Justice, Civil Rights Division, *Title VI Legal Manual* (Updated), "Section VII: Proving Discrimination—Disparate Impact," https://www.justice.gov/crt/fcs/T6Manual7.
17 Heather Mac Donald, *When Race Trumps Merit: How the Pursuit of Equity Sacrifices Excellence, Destroys Beauty, and Threatens Lives* (DW Books, 2023).
18 John McWhorter, *Woke Racism: How a New Religion Has Betrayed Black America* (Portfolio/Penguin, 2021), 16.
19 LeanIn.Org and McKinsey & Company, *Women in the Workplace 2024: The 10th Anniversary Report*, https://womenintheworkplace.com.
20 Jennifer Hochschild, "Affirmative Action as Culture War," in *The Cultural Territories of Race: Black and White Boundaries*, ed. Michèle Lamont (University of Chicago Press, 1999), 353.
21 "Affirmative Action," in *Merriam-Webster Dictionary*, https://www.merriam-webster.com/dictionary/affirmative%20action.
22 Exec. Order No. 10925, 3 C.F.R. 86, Section 301 (March 6, 1961).
23 Lyndon B. Johnson, "To Fulfill These Rights," commencement address, Howard University, June 4, 1965.
24 Johnson, "To Fulfill These Rights."
25 Melvin I. Urofsky, *The Affirmative Action Puzzle: A Living History from Reconstruction to Today* (Pantheon, 2020), xi.
26 Grutter v. Bollinger, 539 U.S. 306 (2003), 342–43.
27 Pamela Paul, "A 1991 Book Was Stunningly Prescient About Affirmative Action," *New York Times*, May 26, 2023.

28 Michele Norris, *Our Hidden Conversations: What Americans Really Think About Race and Identity* (Simon & Schuster, 2024), xxxiii.

29 California Constitution, Article I: Declaration of Rights, Section 31(a), https://law.justia.com/constitution/california/article-i/section-31/.

30 Pew Research Center, "The American Middle Class is Losing Ground," December 9, 2015, https://www.pewresearch.org/social-trends/2015/12/09/the-american-middle-class-is-losing-ground/.

31 Stephen L. Carter, *Reflections of an Affirmative Action Baby*, quoted in Pamela Paul, "1991 Book Was Stunningly Prescient About Affirmative Action."

32 Jason I. Riley, "Glenn Loury's Story Shows How Not to Help," *Wall Street Journal*, June 4, 2024.

33 STARS College Network, "New College Network Builds Support for Students in Rural and Small-Town America," April 4, 2023, https://engage.starscollegenetwork.org.

34 Bennett Leckrone, "College Network to Support Rural Students Expands," Best Colleges, August 16, 2024, https://www.bestcolleges.com/news/stars-network-expands/.

35 Lincoln Quillian, Devah Pager, Ole Hexel, and Arnfinn H. Midtbøen, "Meta-Analysis of Field Experiments Shows No Change in Racial Discrimination in Hiring Over Time," *Proceedings of the National Academy of Sciences* 114, no. 41 (2017): 10870-75.

36 Ashley Jardina, Peter Q. Blair, Justin Heck, and Papia Debroy, "The Limits of Educational Attainment in Mitigating Occupational Segregation Between Black and White Workers," *National Bureau of Economic Research Working Paper* No. 31641, August 2023.

37 Students for Fair Admissions, Inc. v. President and Fellows of Harvard College and SFFA v. University of North Carolina, 600 U.S. 181 (2023).

38 Lee C. Bollinger and Geoffrey R. Stone, *A Legacy of Discrimination: The Essential Constitutionality of Affirmative Action* (Oxford University Press, 2023), 120.

39 US Department of Justice, Civil Rights Division, and US Department of Education, "Dear Colleague Letter on the Supreme Court's Decision Regarding Race in Admissions," August 14, 2023, https://www.ed.gov/media/document/colleague-20230814pdf.

40 Vanessa Huber and Christopher Lucca, "Federal Court Declines to Extend Affirmative Action Decision into Military Academy Admissions," Clark Hill, December 23, 2024, https://www.clarkhill.com/news-events/news/federal-court-declines-to-extend-sffa-decision-into-military-academy-admissions/.

41 US Department of Education, *Strategies for Increasing Diversity and Opportunity in Higher Education*, September 2023.

42 Anemona Hartocollis and Stephanie Saul, "End of Affirmative Action Yields Puzzling Class Data," *New York Times*, September 14, 2024, A13.

43 Hartocollis and Saul, "End of Affirmative Action."

44 Jason L. Riley, "Some Colleges Dodge the Affirmative Action Ruling," *Wall Street Journal*, September 24, 2024, quoting John Yoo.

45 Anemona Hartocollis, "Yale, Princeton and Duke Are Questioned Over Decline in Asian Students," *Wall Street Journal*, September 17, 2024.

46 Students for Fair Admissions, Inc. v. University of North Carolina, Brief for Respondent-Students, No. 21-707, filed July 25, 2022, at Introduction, https://www.supremecourt.gov/DocketPDF/21/21-707/230788/20220725145945750_Respondent%20Students%20Merits%20Brief.pdf.

47 Lauren Weber, "Doctoral Program Is Latest to Be Challenged over Diversity Efforts," *Wall Street Journal*, August 29, 2024, A3.

48 Code of Federal Regulations, Title 34, Subtitle B, Chapter VI, Part 647, https://www.ecfr.gov/current/title-34/subtitle-B/chapter-VI/part-647; Weber, "Doctoral Program Is Latest to Be Challenged over Diversity Efforts."

49 Young Americans for Freedom et al. v. US Department of Education and Miguel Cardona, Order Denying Motion for Preliminary Injunction, US District Court for the District of North Dakota, filed December 31, 2024.

50 Kris W. Kobach, Jonathan Skrmetti, Steve Marshall, Tim Griffin, Todd Rokita, Brenna Bird, Daniel Cameron, Lynn Fitch, Mike Hilgers, Alan Wilson, Patrick Morrisey, Andrew Bailey, and Austin Knudsen, letter to Fortune 100 CEOs regarding race-based employment and contracting practices, July 13, 2023, https://www.tn.gov/content/dam/tn/attorneygeneral/documents/pr/2023/pr23-27-letter.pdf.

51 James C. Davis, John Cromartie, Tracey Farrigan, Brandon Genetin, Austin Sanders, and Justin B. Winikoff, *Rural America at a Glance: 2023 Edition*, US Department of Agriculture, Economic Research Service, November 2023.

52 Aaron D. Ford, Kris Mayes, Rob Bonta, Philip J. Weiser, William Tong, Kathy Jennings, Brian Schwalb, Anne Lopez, Kwame Raoul, Aaron M. Frey, Anthony Brown, Andrea Campbell, Dana Nessel, Keith Ellison, Matt Platkin, Raúl Torrez, Letitia James, Ellen Rosenblum,

Peter Neronha, Charity Clark, and Bob Ferguson, letter to Fortune 100 CEOs supporting diversity, equity, and inclusion initiatives, July 19, 2023, https://ag.nv.gov/uploadedFiles/ag.nv.gov/Content/News/PR/PR_Docs/2022(1)/Fortune%20100%20Letter%207.19.23.pdf.

53 US Equal Employment Opportunity Commission, "Statement from EEOC Chair Charlotte A. Burrows on Supreme Court Ruling on College Affirmative Action Programs," press release, June 29, 2023, https://www.eeoc.gov/newsroom/statement-eeoc-chair-charlotte-burrows-supreme-court-ruling-college-affirmative-action.

54 Te-Ping Chen and Lauren Weber, "The Rise and Fall of the Chief Diversity Officer," *Wall Street Journal*, July 21, 2023.

55 Ruth Simons and Theo Francis, "Companies Are Scrapping or Rolling Back DEI Grants," *Wall Street Journal*, October 10, 2024.

56 Patrick Coffee, "Marketers Maintain Focus on Diversity Despite Outside Pressures," *Wall Street Journal*, September 25, 2023.

57 Vivian Hunt, Dennis Layton, and Sara Prince, *Why Diversity Matters*, McKinsey & Company, January 2015.

58 Jeffrey Baumgartner, "Why Diversity Is the Mother of Creativity," *Innovation Management*, November 24, 2010, https://innovationmanagement.se/2010/11/24/why-diversity-is-the-mother-of-creativity/.

59 Kate Zernike, *The Exceptions: Nancy Hopkins, MIT, and the Fight for Women in Science* (Scribner, 2023).

60 Coqual, *Being Black in Corporate America*, 2019, https://coqual.org/reports/being-black-in-corporate-america-an-intersectional-exploration/.

61 Jennifer Miller, "Why Some Companies Are Saying 'Diversity and Belonging' Instead of 'Diversity and Inclusion,'" *New York Times*, May 5, 2023.

62 Joseph Epstein, "The Tyranny of Diversity," *Wall Street Journal*, December 31, 2020, A13.

63 David French, "What University Presidents Got Right and Wrong About Antisemitic Speech," *New York Times*, December 10, 2023.

64 Ilya Shapiro, "DEI at Law Schools Could Bring Down America," interview by Tunku Varadarajan, *Wall Street Journal*, March 28, 2023.

65 Theo Francis and Melanie Evans, "Fight Against DEI Shifts to Medical Care," *Wall Street Journal*, August 15, 2023, A3.

66 Wells Fargo, Form 10-Q for the Quarterly Period Ended June 30, 2024, Note 10 to the Financial Statements; Isaiah Poritz, "Wells Fargo to Face Securities Suit over Sham Job Interviews," *Bloomberg Law*, July

29, 2024, https://news.bloomberglaw.com/litigation/wells-fargo-to-face-securities-suit-over-sham-job-interviews.

67 Lauren Cromie, "SHRM Removes Equity from DEI," *EverythingPeople This Week!*, July 16, 2024, https://www.aseonline.org/News-Events/ASE-News/EverythingPeople-This-Week/shrm-removes-equity-from-dei.

68 Steven Levitsky and Daniel Ziblatt, *Tyranny of the Minority* (Crown, 2023) 4.

69 Pauline R. Clance and Suzanne A. Imes, "The Imposter Phenomenon in High Achieving Women: Dynamics and Therapeutic Intervention," *Psychotherapy: Theory, Research and Practice* 15, no. 3 (1978).

70 Ashley Abramson, "How to Overcome Imposter Phenomenon," *Monitor on Psychology* 52, no. 4 (June 2021), https://www.apa.org/monitor/2021/06/cover-impostor-phenomenon.

CHAPTER FOUR

1 Gordon Hardy, "Why Give? Religious Roots of Charity," Harvard Divinity School News Archive, first published December 12, 2013.

2 Rob Reich, *Just Giving: Why Philanthropy Is Failing Democracy and How It Can Do Better* (Princeton, 2019), 8–9 and chap. 3.

3 Jodie Shaw, "How the 'Merchant of Death' Turned Patron of Peace," *Medium*, January 12, 2017, https://medium.com/thrive-global/how-the-merchant-of-death-turned-patron-of-peace-and-what-that-means-to-you-c780d84c04b5.

4 David W. Chen and Michael Corkery, "A New Playbook for College Donors: Power Politics," *New York Times*, December 13, 2023.

5 Robert D. McFadden, "Charles Feeney, Who Made a Fortune and Then Gave It Away, Dies at 92," *New York Times*, October 13, 2023.

6 Reich, *Just Giving*, 10.

7 Jo Littler, *Against Meritocracy: Culture, Power and Myths of Mobility* (Routledge, 2018), 219.

8 Stephen J. McNamee, *The Meritocracy Myth*, 4th ed. (Rowman & Littlefield, 2018), 217.

9 Adrian Wooldridge, *The Aristocracy of Talent: How Meritocracy Made the Modern World* (Skyhorse Publishing, 2021), 376.

10 Reich, *Just Giving*, 7.

11 Andrew Carnegie, "The Gospel of Wealth," 1889, https://media.carnegie.org/filer_public/ab/c9/abc9fb4b-dc86-4ce8-ae31-a983b9a326ed/ccny_essay_1889_thegospelofwealth.pdf.

12 Ross Douthat, "Why the Right and the Left Hate Kenneth Griffin's Huge Gift to Harvard," *New York Times*, April 14, 2023.

CHAPTER FIVE

1 Stephen J. McNamee, *The Meritocracy Myth*, 4th ed. (Rowman & Littlefield, 2018), 208.

2 Robert H. Frank, *Success and Luck: Good Fortune and the Myth of Meritocracy* (Princeton University Press, 2016), 118ff. and app. 2.

3 Daniel Markovits, *The Meritocracy Trap: How America's Foundational Myth Feeds Inequality, Dismantles the Middle Class, and Devours the Elite* (Penguin Press, 2019), 277.

4 Markovits, *Meritocracy Trap*, 279.

5 Jo Littler, *Against Meritocracy: Culture, Power and Myths of Mobility* (Routledge, 2018), 217, 219.

6 Anand Giridharadas, *Winners Take All: The Elite Charade of Changing the World* (Knopf, 2018), 10.

7 Vivek Ramaswamy, *Woke, Inc.: Inside the Corporate Social Justice Scam* (Swift, 2022), 3–4.

8 Barton Swaim, "'Milton Friedman' Review: America's Anti-Economist," *Wall Street Journal*, November 27, 2023.

9 "Evaluating the Success of the Great Society," *Washington Post*, May 17, 2014, https://www.washingtonpost.com/wp-srv/special/national/great-society-at-50/.

10 Peggy Noonan, "So You Think You Want a Political Fighter?," *Wall Street Journal*, November 17, 2023.

11 Robert Draper, "Departing House Members Ask: 'Why Am I Here?,'" *New York Times*, May 30, 2024.

12 For example, Tamara Keith, "When Politicians Have No Shame, the Old Rules Don't Apply," NPR, February 15, 2023, https://www.npr.org/2023/02/15/1157049312/george-santos-politics-of-shame.

13 Edelman, *2023 Edelman Trust Barometer Global Report*, March 2023, https://www.edelman.com/sites/g/files/aatuss191/files/2023-03/2023%20Edelman%20Trust%20Barometer%20Global%20Report%20FINAL.pdf.

14 Pew Research Center, "Public Trust in Government: 1958–2023," September 19, 2023, https://www.pewresearch.org/politics/2023/09/19/public-trust-in-government-1958-2023/.

15 Bernie Marcus, "Entrepreneurship Will Lift Minorities Up," *Wall Street Journal*, January 10, 2023, A15.

16 Matthew Desmond, *Poverty, by America* (Crown, 2023), 123.

CHAPTER SIX

1 McKinsey & Company, "Our Approach," *2021 ESG Report*, https://www.mckinsey.com/about-us/social-responsibility/2021-esg-report/overview.

2 Linda Greenhouse, "Ruth Bader Ginsburg, Supreme Court's Feminist Icon, Is Dead at 87," *New York Times*, September 24, 2020.

3 Eli Wald, "The Rise and Fall of the WASP and Jewish Firms," *Stanford Law Review* 60 (2008): 1804–05.

4 Jerold S. Auerbach, "Don't Call Us. We'll Call You," *New York Times*, April 13, 1976.

5 William Overend, "Leading Law Firms—a History of Minority Bias," *Los Angeles Times*, September 28, 1987.

6 Adam Liptak, "The Road to a Supreme Court Clerkship Starts at Three Ivy League Colleges," *New York Times*, February 6, 2023.

7 Sidley Austin Prelaw Scholars Program.

8 ABA Young Lawyers Division, "Best Practices for Legal Diversity Programs," August 11, 2023, https://www.americanbar.org/events-cle/ecd/ondemand/433237895/.

9 Bryan Strickland, "Employers Embrace Apprenticeship Program for Finance Business Partners," *Journal of Accountancy*, November 14, 2022, https://www.journalofaccountancy.com/news/2022/nov/employers-embrace-apprenticeship-program-finance-business-partners.html.

10 Bryan Strickland, "AICPA Apprenticeship Program Receives Grant from Maryland Department of Labor," *Journal of Accountancy*, September 21, 2022.

11 Office of Senator Tom Cotton, "Cotton Warns Top Law Firms About Race-Based Hiring Practices," press release, July 17, 2023, https://www.cotton.senate.gov/news/press-releases/cotton-warns-top-law-firms-about-race-based-hiring-practices.

12 Daniel Markovits, *The Meritocracy Trap: How America's Foundational Myth Feeds Inequality, Dismantles the Middle Class, and Devours the Elite* (Penguin Press, 2019), x, xxii.

13 Andrew Maloney, "In Era of Disengagement, How Do Law Firms Motivate Lawyers and Staff," *American Lawyer*, June 26, 2023, https://law.com/americanlawyer/2023/06/26/in-era-of-disengagement-what-can-law-firms-do-to-motivate-lawyers-and-staff/?slreturn=2024122823411.

14 Bruce Feiler, "The New Rules of Success in a Post-career World," *Wall Street Journal*, June 3–4, 2023, C1.

15 Sarah Chaney Cambon and Paul Hannon, "Work on Gender Gaps Earns Economics Nobel," *Wall Street Journal*, October 10, 2023, A2.

16 National Association for Law Placement, "Women and People of Color in U.S. Law Firms," *NALP Bulletin+*, March 2024, https://www.nalp.org/0324research.

17 National Football League, "NFL Owners Pass Resolution Rewarding Teams for Developing Minority Coaches, Execs," November 10, 2020, https://www.nfl.com/news/nfl-owners-pass-resolution-rewarding-teams-for-developing-minority-coaches-execs.

18 Jeff Benedict, "Why Bill Belichick's Genius Can't Be Replicated," *New York Times*, January 12, 2024.

19 NFL (@NFL), "We, the NFL, condemn racism and the systematic oppression of Black People. We, the NFL, admit we were wrong for not listening to NFL players earlier and encourage all to speak out and peacefully protest. We, the NFL, believe Black Lives Matter. #InspireChange," X (formerly Twitter), June 5, 2020, https://x.com/NFL/status/1269034074552721408.

CHAPTER SEVEN

1 Drucker Institute, "The 2024 Methodology for the Drucker Institute's Company Rankings," https://drucker.institute/2024-methology-for-the-drucker-institutes-company-rank.

2 Thomas A. Cole, *CEO Leadership: Navigating the New Era in Corporate Governance* (University of Chicago Press, 2019).

3 William T. Allen, "Our Schizophrenic Conception of the Business Corporation," *Cardozo Law Review* 14 (1992): 261.

4 Milton Friedman, "The Social Responsibility of Business Is to Increase Its Profits," *New York Times Magazine*, September 13, 1970.

5 Linda Qiu, "No, 'Wokeness' Did Not Cause Silicon Valley Bank's Collapse," *New York Times*, March 15, 2023, quoting a Ron DeSantis interview on Fox News, among others.

6 David Ingram, "Elon Musk Criticized by Civil Rights Groups over Claim That Diversity Efforts Make Flying Less Safe," NBC News, January 11, 2024, https://www.nbcnews.com/tech/internet/elon-musk-boeing-dei-diversity-x-posts-pilots-rcna133351.

7 Tarini Parti and Alex Leary, "Without Evidence, Trump Blames DEI for Crash," *Wall Street Journal*, January 31, 2025, A4.

8 Gerard Baker, "If Western Civilization Dies, Put It Down as a Suicide," *Wall Street Journal*, April 17, 2023.

9 Jesus Jimenez, "Why Chick-fil-A Is Drawing Fire Over a 'Culture of Belonging,'" *New York Times*, May 31, 2023.

10 Richard F. Lacaille, Global Chief Investment Officer of State Street Global Advisors, "Dear Board Chair: Diversity Strategy, Goals and Disclosure: Our Expectations for Public Companies," letter dated August 27, 2020.

11 Black Economic Alliance Foundation, "New Poll by the Black Economic Alliance Foundation/The Harris Poll: Corporate Diversity Initiatives Overwhelmingly Supported Across Racial, Ideological, and Generational Lines," press release, August 28, 2023.

12 Patrick Coffee, "Marketers Maintain Focus on Diversity Despite Outside Pressures," *Wall Street Journal*, September 25, 2023.

13 Costco Wholesale Corporation, *Proxy Statement* dated December 11, 2024, filed with the Securities and Exchange Commission on Schedule 14A, 31–33.

14 Erich Schwartzel and Chip Cutter, "CEOs Kill Policies Before Inauguration," *Wall Street Journal*, January 11–12, 2025, A1.

15 The White House, "Ending Illegal Discrimination and Restoring Merit-Based Opportunity," January 22, 2025, https://www.whitehouse.gov/presidential-actions/2025/01/ending-illegal-discrimination-and-restoring-merit-based-opportunity/.

16 John Deere (@JohnDeere), "Our customers' trust and confidence in us are of the utmost importance to everyone at John Deere. We fully intend to earn it every day and in every way we can." X (formerly Twitter), July 16, 2024, https://x.com/JohnDeere/status/1813318977650847944.

17 Paul Bergeron, "KPMG Survey Shows Most CEOs to Put ESG on Pause," ALM Globest, October 6, 2022, https://www.globest.com/2022/10/06/kpmg-survey-shows-most-ceos-to-put-esg-on-pause/?slreturn=2024122825001.

18 Business Roundtable, "Placing a Greater Emphasis on Skills in Hiring and Advancement, Improving Equity and Diversity in Employment," https://www.businessroundtable.org/workforceskills.

19 Matt Seligman, Joseph Fuller, and Alex Martin, "Skills-Based Hiring: The Long Road from Pronouncements to Practice," Harvard Business School and Burning Glass Institute, February 2024, https://www.hbs.edu/managing-the-future-of-work/Documents/research/Skills-Based%20Hiring.pdf.

20 Sanvi Bangalore, "Students Try to Get a Head Start on Jobs," *Wall Street Journal*, Aug 21, 2024, A9.

21 Callum Borchers and Lindsay Ellis, "The Secrets to a Successful Job Search," *Wall Street Journal*, June 1–2, 2024, B1.

22 US Securities and Exchange Commission, "JP Morgan Chase Paying $264 Million to Settle FCPA Charges," press release, November 17, 2016.

23 Coursera, https://www.coursera.org/.

24 See https://www.pathtopro.com.

25 Ronald J. Daniels, Grant Shreve, and Phillip Spector, *What Universities Owe Democracy* (Johns Hopkins, 2021), 71–72.

26 Kate King, "Short-Staffed Hotels Offer Career Growth to Hire Employees," *Wall Street Journal*, March 21, 2023.

27 Boris Groysberg, *Chasing Stars: The Myth of Talent and the Portability of Performance* (Princeton University Press, 2010).

28 National Association of Corporate Directors, *Report of the NACD Blue Ribbon Commission on Talent Development*, October 2013.

29 Coqual, *Being Black in Corporate America*, 2019, https://coqual.org/reports/being-black-in-corporate-america-an-intersectional-exploration/.

30 Andrew Ramonas, "Nasdaq Board Diversity Rules Face State Attorneys General Probe," *Bloomberg Law*, October 3, 2024.

31 Thomas A. Cole, "Supporting Black Leaders in Corporate America," 2020, Directors & Boards, https://www.directorsandboards.com/board-composition/board-diversity/singlesupporting-black-leaders-corporate-america/.

32 Thomas A. Cole, "Business and Politics: When Should Companies Take a Public Position?," Harvard Law School Forum on Corporate Governance, May 6, 2021, https://corpgov.law.harvard.edu/2021/05/06/business-and-politics-when-should-companies-take-a-public-position/.

33 John Gardner, *On Leadership* (Free Press, 1993), chap. 2.

34 Daniel Goleman, "Leadership That Gets Results," *Harvard Business Review*, March–April 2000, 82–83.

35 Steven N. Kaplan and Morten Sorensen, "Are CEOs Different?," *Journal of Finance*, March 9, 2021; Emily Borrow, "The Moral Hazards of Being Beautiful," *Wall Street Journal*, June 10–11, 2023.

36 Michael C. Jensen and William H. Meckling, "Theory of the Firm: Managerial Behavior, Agency Costs and Ownership Structure," *Journal of Financial Economics* (October 1976), ssrn.com/abstract=94043.

37 Meghan Daniels, "Why Your Kid Might Not Be the Best CEO for the Family Business," *Axial*, September 15, 2015, https://www.axial.net/forum/why-your-kid-might-not-be-the-best-ceo-for-the-family-business/.

CHAPTER EIGHT

1 Spencer Stuart, *2022 S&P 500 CEO Transitions*, February 2023.

2 The University of Chicago Graham School, Continuing Liberal and Professional Studies, "Leadership & Society Initiative," 2023, https://leadforsociety.uchicago.edu/; email from Dean of Graham School, Seth Green, September 6, 2023.

3 Toni Hoy, "Mission Creep: How Nonprofits Can Stay True to Their Missions," *Board Effect*, December 7, 2022, https://www.boardeffect.com/blog/mission-creep/.

4 Mary Churchill, "The SAT and ACT Are Less Important than You Might Think," *Inside Higher Ed*, January 29, 2023.

5 Ronald J. Daniels, Grant Shreve, and Phillip Spector, *What Universities Owe Democracy* (Johns Hopkins, 2021), 62.

6 Michael D. Shear and Anemona Hartocollis, "Education Dept. Opens Civil Rights Inquiry into Harvard's Legacy Admissions," *New York Times*, July 25, 2023.

7 Janet Lorin and *Bloomberg*, "Harvard and Other Wealthy Massachusetts Schools with Legacy Admissions Hit with Proposal That Would Raise Hundreds of Millions," *Fortune*, July 5, 2023, https://fortune.com/2023/07/05/harvard-legacy-admissions-wealthy-massachusetts-schools-tax-proposal/; An Act to Advance Fairness, Integrity, and Excellence in Higher Education Admissions, H.R. 3760, 193rd Gen. Ct. (Mass. 2023), https://malegislature.gov/Bills/193/H3760.Html.

8 Blake Jones, "Why Legacy Admissions Have Exploded in the US," *Politico*, October 10, 2024.

9 Equal Protection Project of the Legal Insurrection Foundation, to the US Department of Education, Office for Civil Rights, "Civil Rights Complaint Against Kansas State University for Its Racially Discriminatory 'Joey Lee Garmon Undergraduate Multicultural Student Scholarship,'" August 16, 2023, https://static.foxnews.com/foxnews.com/content/uploads/2023/08/OCR-Complaint-Kansas-State-University.pdf.

10 US Department of Justice, Civil Rights Division, and US Department of Education, "Dear Colleague Letter on the Supreme Court's Decision Regarding Race in Admissions," August 14, 2023, https://www.ed.gov/media/document/colleague-20230814pdf.

11 James Huffman, "How the Diversity Mission Has Limited Free Expression on Campus," *Law & Liberty*, May 15, 2019, https://lawliberty.org/how-the-diversity-mission-has-limited-free-expression-on-campus/.

12 Gallup, *The First Amendment on Campus 2020 Report: College Students' Views of Free Expression*, Knight Foundation, 2020, https://knightfoundation.org/reports/the-first-amendment-on-campus-2020-report-college-students-views-of-free-expression/.

13 Christopher L. Eisgruber, "Why Mutual Respect Makes Free Speech Better," *The Daily Princetonian*, July 20, 2020.

14 John Palfrey, "No Light Between Diversity and Free Expression," *New York Times*, June 22, 2016.

15 Faculty, Alumni, and Students Opposed to Racial Preferences v. Northwestern University et al., Complaint filed July 2, 2024, https://fingfx.thomsonreuters.com/gfx/legaldocs/akveoobrgvr/northwestern%20(1).pdf.

16 Michael Bloomberg, "Harvard Commencement Address," May 29, 2014, quoted in *Wall Street Journal*, "Notable & Quotable," May 30,2014.

17 Aiyana G. White and Tyler J. VanderWeele, "Higher Education Has a Viewpoint Diversity Problem. Here's How to Respond," *The Harvard Crimson*, February 12, 2024, https://www.thecrimson.com/column/council-on-academic-freedom-at-harvard/article/2024/2/12/VanderWeele-harvard-viewpoint-diversity/.

18 An Act Relating to Higher Education, S. 266, 2023 Leg., Reg. Sess. (Fla. 2023) (enacted); Relating to Diversity, Equity, and Inclusion Initiatives at Public Institutions of Higher Learning, S. 17, 88th Leg., Reg. Sess. (Tex. 2023), effective Jan. 1, 2024.

19 An Act Relating to Diversity, Equity, and Inclusion, S. 129, 2023 Leg., Reg. Sess. (Ala. 2023).

20 Christopher F. Rufo, Ilya Shapiro, and Matt Beienburg, *Abolish DEI Bureaucracies and Restore Colorblind Equality in Public Universities*, Manhattan Institute, January 2023.

21 Henry Stone, "How Colleges and Universities Get Around State DEI Bans," *Wall Street Journal*, December 21–23, 2024, A11.

22 Higher Education Enhancement Act, S. 83, 135th Gen. Assemb. (Ohio 2023).

23 Laura Lanese, letter to State Senator Jerry Cirino (sponsor of Ohio SB 83), May 18, 2023, Inter-university Council of Ohio, https://iuc-ohio.org/2023/05/18/iuc-sb-83-to-senator-jerry-cirino/.

24 Andrew Delbanco, "Great Books Can Heal Our Divided Campuses," *Wall Street Journal*, June 10–11, 2023, C1.

25 Debra Satz and Dan Edelstein, "By Abandoning Civics, Colleges Helped Create the Culture Wars," *New York Times*, September 3, 2023.

26 Melissa Eddy, "A New Place to Learn Civics: The Workplace," *New York Times*, October 29, 2023.

27 Dana Goldstein, "For Republican Governors, Civics Is the Latest Educational Battleground," *New York Times*, November 30, 2023.

28 Barton Swaim, "UNC Tries to Create a 'Free-Speech Culture,'" *Wall Street Journal*, October 5–6, 2024.

29 Debra Satz and Dan Edelstein, "By Dropping Civics, Colleges Gave Fuel to the Culture Wars," *New York Times*, September 7, 2023, A26.

30 Isabella Glassman, "Careerism is Ruining College," *New York Times*, September 24, 2024.

31 Frank Bruni, "The Unsung Alma Maters," chap.1 in *Where You Go Is Not Who You'll Be: An Antidote to the College Admissions Mania* (Grand Central Publishing, 2016), 184.

32 Francesca Mari, "What Do Students at Elite Colleges Really Want?," *New York Times*, May 22, 2024.

33 Richard Arum and Mitchell L. Stevens, "For Most College Students, Affirmative Action Was Never Enough," *New York Times*, July 3, 2023.

34 Rosa Brooks, "Competence Is Critical for Democracy. Let's Redefine It," *New York Times*, August 15, 2021.

35 Eric F. Goldman, "The Presidency as Moral Leadership," *The Annals of the American Academy of Political and Social Science* (March 1952).

36 Thomas Friedman, "How We've Lost Our Moorings as a Society," *New York Times*, May 28, 2024, quoting Dov Seidman.

37 Southern Baptist Convention, "Resolution on Moral Character of Public Officials," adopted June 1, 1998, https://www.sbc.net/resource-library/resolutions/resolution-on-moral-character-of-public-officials/.

38 Frank Newport, "Religious Group Voting and the 2020 Election," Polling Matters, Gallup, November 13, 2020, https://news.gallup.com/opinion/polling-matters/324410/religious-group-voting-2020-election.aspx.

39 Tim Alberta, *The Kingdom, the Power, and the Glory: American Evangelicals in an Age of Extremism* (Harper, 2023), 24.

40 Trump v. United States, 603 U.S. ___ (2024).

41 Christopher DeMuth, "How Congress Unleashed the Presidency," *Wall Street Journal*, October 26–27, 2024.

42 Sofia Gross and Ashley Spillane, "Civic Responsibility: The Power of Companies to Increase Voter Turnout," Ash Center for Democratic Governance and Innovation/Harvard Kennedy School, June 1, 2019, https://ash.harvard.edu/resources/civic-responsibility-the-power-of-companies-to-increase-voter-turnout/.

43 Wesleyan University, "Democracy 2024," https://www.wesleyan.edu/d2024/.

44 William H. Honan, "Roman L. Hruska Dies at 94," *New York Times*, April 27, 1999.

45 National Education Association, "Issue Explainer: Early Childhood Education," December 2, 2021, https://www.nea.org/advocating-for-change/action-center/our-issues/early-childhood-education.

46 Sara Randazzo, "More Elite Prep Schools Are Offering a Free Ride for the Middle Class," *Wall Street Journal*, September 12, 2024.

47 Richard D. Kahlenberg, "Only Zoning Reform Can Solve America's Housing Crisis," *Wall Street Journal*, June 24–25, 2023, C3.

48 School of Education of American University, "Inequality in Public School Funding: Key Issues & Solutions for Closing the Gap," blog, September 10, 2020, https://soeonline.american.edu/blog/inequality-in-public-school-funding/.

49 Matthew Desmond, *Poverty, by America* (Crown, 2023), 116.

50 Erica E. Meade, "Overview of Community Characteristics in Areas with Concentrated Poverty," Department of Health and Human Services Research Brief, May 2014.

CHAPTER NINE

1 Vivian Hunt, Dennis Layton, and Sara Prince, *Why Diversity Matters*, McKinsey & Company, January 2015.

2 James Mackintosh, "Diversity Was Supposed to Make Us Rich. Not So Much," *Wall Street Journal*, June 28, 2024.

3 Thomas A. Cole, *CEO Leadership: Navigating the New Era in Corporate Governance* (University of Chicago Press, 2019), 5, and sources cited therein.

4 Jonathan Levy, *Ages of American Capitalism: A History of the United States* (Random House, 2022), 631.

5 Chang-Tai Hsieh, Erik Hurst, Charles I. Jones, and Peter Klenow, "The Allocation of Talent and U.S. Economic Growth," *Econometrica* (2019).

6 Wally Adeyemo, blog post, September 2021, quoted in US Department of Treasury, "Racial Inequality in the United States," press release, July 21, 2022, https://home.treasury.gov/news/featured-stories/racial-inequality-in-the-united-states.

7 Elijah Anderson, "Black Success, White Backlash," *The Atlantic*, November 2023.

8 Bob Dylan, "Like a Rolling Stone," *Highway 61 Revisited*, Columbia Records, 1965.

INDEX